T0339472

Cambridge Elements ≡

Elements in Ancient East Asia

ENVIRONMENTS: Interaction Zones of Ancient East Asia

edited by
Erica Fox Brindley
Pennsylvania State University
Rowan Kimon Flad
Harvard University

BRONZE AGE MARITIME AND WARRIOR DYNAMICS IN ISLAND EAST ASIA

Mark Hudson

Max Planck Institute for the Science of Human History

CAMBRIDGE
UNIVERSITY PRESS

CAMBRIDGE
UNIVERSITY PRESS

University Printing House, Cambridge CB2 8BS, United Kingdom

One Liberty Plaza, 20th Floor, New York, NY 10006, USA

477 Williamstown Road, Port Melbourne, VIC 3207, Australia

314–321, 3rd Floor, Plot 3, Splendor Forum, Jasola District Centre, New Delhi – 110025, India

103 Penang Road, #05–06/07, Visioncrest Commercial, Singapore 238467

Cambridge University Press is part of the University of Cambridge.

It furthers the University's mission by disseminating knowledge in the pursuit of education, learning, and research at the highest international levels of excellence.

www.cambridge.org
Information on this title: www.cambridge.org/9781108987318
DOI: 10.1017/9781108982955

© Mark Hudson 2022

First published 2022

A catalogue record for this publication is available from the British Library.

ISBN 978-1-108-98731-8 Paperback
ISSN 2632-7325 (online)
ISSN 2632-7317 (print)

Cambridge University Press has no responsibility for the persistence or accuracy of URLs for external or third-party internet websites referred to in this publication and does not guarantee that any content on such websites is, or will remain, accurate or appropriate.

Bronze Age Maritime and Warrior Dynamics in Island East Asia

Elements in Ancient East Asia

DOI: 10.1017/9781108982955
First published online: March 2022

Mark Hudson
Max Planck Institute for the Science of Human History
Author for correspondence: Mark Hudson, hudson@shh.mpg.de

Abstract: Recent interdisciplinary studies, combining scientific techniques such as ancient DNA analysis with humanistic re-evaluations of the transcultural value of bronze, have presented archaeologists with a fresh view of the Bronze Age in Europe. The new research emphasises long-distance connectivities and political decentralisation. 'Bronzisation' is discussed as a type of proto-globalisation. In this Element, Mark Hudson examines whether these approaches can also be applied to East Asia. Focusing primarily on Island East Asia, he analyses trade, maritime interactions and warrior culture in a comparative Eurasian framework. He argues that the international division of labour associated with Bronze Age trade provided an important stimulus to the rise of decentralised complexity in regions peripheral to alluvial states. Building on James Scott's work, the concept of the 'barbarian niche' is proposed as a way to model the longue durée of premodern Eurasian history. This title is also available as open access on Cambridge Core.

Keywords: Bronze Age, bronzisation, Island East Asia, trade, warfare

ISBNs: 9781108987318 (PB), 9781108982955 (OC)
ISSNs: 2632-7325 (online), ISSN 2632-7317 (print)

Contents

1 Introduction

In recent years, European archaeologists have begun to develop a new view of the Bronze Age, one which emphasises long-distance trade, transport and connectivity. Such ideas are not completely novel but, compared to even ten years ago, we have a much deeper understanding of how people, things and ideas were circulating. Studies of ancient DNA have shown that a large migration into central Europe from the western steppes occurred in the third millennium BC (Haak et al. 2015). Trade had long been considered an important element of the Bronze Age world. Childe (1930) stressed that the production of bronze required the exchange of tin, lead and copper – metals which were only found in certain limited places – but new research has explored the social and cultural meanings of this trade. Vandkilde (2016) coined the term *bronzisation* as a way to emphasise the processes by which bronze formed a *transculture* across Europe and beyond. A transculture can be understood as engagements with the world which encourage meanings transcending place of origin; those meanings can be quite different but share a certain unity in diversity (Vandkilde 2014; Autiero & Cobb 2021).

The darker side of Bronze Age society has also come into clearer focus. In a recent essay, Molloy and Horn (2020: 117) write that 'The transformation of warfare in the Bronze Age was perhaps the most profound transformation in human history.' They go on to explain how new weapons such as swords, shields and body armour established ways of fighting which remained little changed for millennia thereafter. These technical changes were associated with a new sociality of violence and it has been argued that warriors formed a type of Bronze Age 'craft specialist' (Molloy 2017). Since 2008, excavations in the Tollense valley in north-east Germany have uncovered a Bronze Age battlefield dated to circa 1300–1250 BC and which involved fighting between as many as two thousand combatants, implying that armies already existed by the late second millennium BC (Molloy & Horn 2020: 134). Bronze cylinders found at Tollense may have been the personal belongings of a warrior who came from far to the south, suggesting that the battle was part of a supra-regional conflict (Uhlig et al. 2019). A stable isotope study also found evidence for a diverse, non-local group of warriors at Tollense (Price et al. 2019). Growing violence in Bronze Age Europe may have been associated with the spread of steppe pastoralists (Schroeder et al. 2019), leading *New Scientist* magazine to ask: 'were the Yamnaya the most murderous people in history?' (Barras 2019).

New ideas about long-distance interaction during the Bronze Age recall debates some years ago over ancient world systems (Frank 1993; Sherratt

1993; Ratnagar 2001). In my previous research I also made use of world systems theory (Hudson 1999, 2004). However, while previous writings on ancient world systems saw core/periphery relations as *determining* economic dependency and 'underdevelopment', the relationship between core and periphery in the Bronze Age seems to be much more fluid than originally conceived. The fact that sources of tin, copper and lead were limited – and geographically marginal to centres of power in the Near East and eastern Mediterranean – gave the 'barbarians' of the periphery a new dynamism. In some regions, the economic power of the periphery continued long after the Bronze Age and Scott (2017) has dubbed the period from the Bronze Age until around 1600 the 'Golden Age of the Barbarians'. I use the term 'barbarian niche' to emphasise the new opportunities for trade available to non-state peoples from the Bronze Age onwards (Hudson 2019, 2020a).

The 'barbarian niche' is a deliberately tongue-in-cheek way of thinking about a more interconnected and 'democratic' Bronze Age, and is thus also a critique of state-centric views of the past. The idea of the barbarian niche suggests broad similarities in historical processes across Eurasia through the presence of what we might call the 'meta-barbarian'. But to what extent can 'bronzisation' and other concepts developed by European archaeologists actually be applied outside Europe? In this Element I argue that many of the same processes of bronzisation were also at work in eastern Eurasia. This argument is provisional and perhaps at times provocative. In adopting a comparative approach, my intention is not to force East Asia into a European framework. The European research discussed here is itself new and sometimes controversial. Nevertheless, this Element proposes that the historical development of many societies in East Asia from the third millennium BC can be approached as part of a broad, Eurasia-wide process of bronzisation.

1.1 Bronze Transformations

One way to begin to explain the perspective adopted here is to note that bronze often engendered 'creative translations' in material culture, expressions which are not easily interpreted through standard typological frameworks (Kristiansen & Larsson 2005: 13; Sofaer, Jørgensen & Choyke 2013). Skeuomorphs – whereby an artefact fabricated in one medium is made to evoke the physical properties of another – are a common Bronze Age phenomenon. Such skeuomorphs should not be seen as inferior or uninventive; often they displayed great artistic creativity and, in this sense, 'bronzisation' was not just about bronze. In China, Shang elites made jade weapons which mimicked bronze yet retained the 'native' power of jade (Rawson 2017). In Korea, Japan and the Russian Far

East, polished stone daggers, which clearly follow metal prototypes, appear before bronze itself. In fact, East Asian societies such as Mumun Korea (1300–400 BC) and Yayoi Japan (1000 BC–AD 250) seem to follow Bronze Age historical trajectories without possessing bronze in their earlier stages.[1] During the Yayoi, material culture sometimes incorporates designs from the preceding Neolithic Jōmon, one example being decorative patterns on bronze bells. This is usually understood as reflecting the continuing influence of Jōmon tradition (Shitara 2014a), but a broader view would be to see Yayoi appropriation of the Jōmon as a new type of transculture, especially as some decorative designs on Final Jōmon pottery already seem to reflect continental influence (Hudson et al. 2021).

In addition to material translations, in European archaeology the expanding world of the Bronze Age has been discussed in terms of trade, warrior aristocracies, pastoralism, migrations, maritime economies, religious institutions and new disease vectors. In this Element I focus particularly on two aspects of this complex transformation – trading/maritime dynamics and warrior aristocracies. As noted already, trade and the international division of labour grew in importance as bronze became the 'economic motor' of a new Eurasian economy (Kristiansen 2018). Trade required political institutions which allowed safe travel over ever greater distances. Trade and travelling are clearly linked to warriors in Bronze Age rock art in Europe (Ling & Toreld 2018). In East Asia, a system of long-distance travel is clear from texts like the *Wei zhi*, a section of which describes western Japan. This Chinese text has received attention mostly for its confusing directions to the kingdom of Yamatai, which supposedly controlled part of Japan at the time (Young 1958; Kidder 2007). Less often remarked upon is how it portrays a world in which traders and envoys could apparently move smoothly across vast areas. While the *Wei zhi* itself dates to the third century AD, the system of travel it describes must have been established much earlier.

The sea was crucial for Bronze Age communications and sailing technologies played a major role in the new connectivities (Broodbank 2010). Less attention has been given to fishing and other economic uses of the sea. In Atlantic Europe, it is argued, there was a sudden decline in the exploitation of marine foods from the onset of the Neolithic (Richards, Schulting & Hedges 2003; Cramp et al. 2014). While there are certainly exceptions to this trend – for example, excavations on Molène island off Brittany have produced evidence for an Early Bronze Age settlement which combined farming, fishing and exchange (Pailler et al. 2019) – a similar argument is sometimes made for parts of East Asia. For

---

[1] For debates over the absolute chronology of the Yayoi period, see Mizoguchi (2013: 33–6).

example, the Jōmon cultures of Japan are well known for their high dependence on the sea, but a significant decline in fishing with the arrival of cereal farming in the archipelago at the beginning of the first millennium BC has been noted (cf. Hudson 2019, 2021a, *in press*). However, there was a new trend towards more *specialised* use of the sea and marine resources in at least parts of East Asia from the third millennium BC. Furthermore, we should not assume that fishing groups never engaged in farming themselves. For too long, archaeologists in East Asia and elsewhere have focussed on 'peasant farmers' (Zvelebil 1995; Amino 2012) but, as discussed below, there is a need to consider alternative models, including what Ling and colleagues (2018) have called the 'maritime mode of production' as discussed in section 2.1.

The recent publication of the *Cambridge World History of Violence* has provided a new, global perspective on this topic, but Bronze Age East Asia is thinly covered in these volumes and in this Element I want to take the opportunity to discuss the region in more depth. Building on Hudson and colleagues (2020), I discuss warfare and violence in Bronze Age Japan in a more comparative framework.

This Element is not an attempt at a synthesis of Bronze Age East Asia. Rather, the text explores maritime and warrior dynamics in Island East Asia in a comparative framework and provides a new 'framing' for the issues it discusses. Given the space limitations of the Element format, the arguments made here are provisional and designed to provoke debate. The author is currently writing a longer work in which a more detailed theoretical basis for these ideas will be presented.

1.2 Bronze Age East Asia: Some Orientations

There are two rather different ways of defining the Bronze Age in East Asia and indeed elsewhere. The traditional way is to look at when bronze actually began to be used in each regional sequence. In some parts of eastern Eurasia this can be quite late. In Korea and Japan, for example, bronze appears around the eighth and fourth centuries BC, respectively (Rhee et al. 2007: 413; Barnes 2015; Fujio 2015: 110). In some places, bronze is introduced at more or less the same time as iron, giving rise to terms like 'Palaeometal Age' in the Russian Far East or 'Metal Age' in Island Southeast Asia.

Another approach is to adopt a more standardised framework incorporating Eurasia as a whole. If the Bronze Age in the Near East began in the late fourth millennium BC and if bronze appeared in western China by 2800 BC (Gansu Provincial Cultural Relics Work Team et al. 1984), then might it not make sense to use the *same* periodisation even if some local areas had not yet adopted bronzeworking? In this approach the Bronze Age becomes a 'world historical epoch' (Kristiansen 2015). In my view this perspective makes a great deal of sense, even for the Japanese islands. While Japan remained one of the most isolated parts of Eurasia in the third millennium BC, many of the changes which occurred there from that time can be understood as a *reaction* to the Bronze Age as a world historical epoch (Hudson et al. 2021).

On a regional scale, the problem of time/space classification is nicely illustrated by debates over Yayoi Japan. In an influential book titled *Two Other Japanese Cultures*, Fujimoto (1988) attempted to classify the prehistoric cultures of Hokkaido and Okinawa as different but still 'Japanese'. At the time, this was an important statement supporting a 'multicultural' identity. Fujimoto proposed three cultural zones located in the north, centre and south of the archipelago; these were separated by intermediate areas which he termed *bokashi* or 'fuzzy' zones (cf. Batten 2003: 72–3). Fujimoto's approach was taken up by Fujio (2013), who defined the Yayoi as a culture based on irrigated wet-rice farming and maintained through 'Yayoi rituals'. Such definitions assume that wet-rice agriculture is the necessary basis of a 'central' Japanese culture. In my view, the great diversity and dynamism of the Yayoi period can be better understood through an approach which places the whole archipelago – and indeed its mainland connections – within the same frame of analysis. A similar perspective on Bronze Age China is adopted by Campbell and colleagues (2021).

Of course it would be unhelpful to insist that one of these two approaches to periodisation is necessarily superior to the other; both describe aspects of the same historical reality. As in medieval studies (Jervis 2017), there is a need for a multi-scalar perspective which considers both the local and the global. Sherratt (2011: 4) reminds us that 'It is the privilege of archaeology to deal with all scales of phenomena, from the global to the local, over timescales from the momentary to the long term.' Furthermore, given our imperfect knowledge of the archaeological record, it can be hard to distinguish between the two approaches. When I was an undergraduate in the 1980s, for example, there was considerable excitement about early dates for bronze in Southeast Asia. Excavations in the mid-1970s at Ban Chiang in Thailand had produced radio-carbon dates which seemed to suggest that bronze had reached mainland Southeast Asia as early as 2000 BC. White and Hamilton (2009) have proposed that this reflects a separate ancestry from bronze in China and can be connected with the Seima–Turbino horizon distributed from Finland to the Altai. A reanalysis found that the early Ban Chiang dates are unreliable, concluding that bronze reached mainland Southeast Asia only around 1000 BC in a context of trade with China in cowrie shells and turtle plastrons (Higham, Higham &

Kijngam 2011). The most recent overview of the bronze chronology of northeast Thailand argues that there is now 'near universal acceptance' for this short chronology (Higham & Cawte 2021). The details of this debate will perhaps continue to be discussed but retain important implications for a broader historical interpretation.

A further problem is how we approach the *end* of the Bronze Age and the transition to the Iron Age. The term 'Iron Age' is rarely used in East Asian archaeology. This is sometimes because there is a very short period after the arrival of bronze before iron is also adopted. In the Primorye province of the Russian Far East, for instance, bronze was introduced around 900 BC and iron some four centuries later around 500 BC (Popov, Zhushchikhovskaya & Nikitin 2019). In Europe, the Iron Age saw a move away from long-distance trade and a new tension between local autonomy and control (Kristiansen 1998; Cunliffe 2008). To some extent the same trend can be seen in East Asia. In the Warring States era (475–221 BC), the Chinese state attempted to prohibit the export of iron to outlying 'barbarians' yet the metal nevertheless spread to Korea and Japan through various non-state actors (Barnes 2007: 65–7). One might say that Japanese society became more autonomous once iron deposits in the archipelago were widely exploited. That did not occur, however, until the late sixth century AD (Fujio 2000: 97; Matsugi 2018); before then, the inhabitants of the Japanese islands obtained iron from the Korean peninsula in a trading system which, *in its economic structure*, was little changed from the Bronze Age. Furthermore, the period when Japan became metallurgically autonomous was one when it was increasingly influenced by new religious and political ideas, notably Confucianism, Buddhism and Taoism (Barnes 2014; Bauer 2017; Deal 2017). The mix of these international ideologies with changing patterns of political and economic centralisation and decentralisation lends the period encompassing Japan's Kofun and 'classical' (Nara–Heian) ages more similarities with what Di Cosmo and Maas (2018) call 'Eurasian Late Antiquity' than with the west Eurasian Iron Age.

However one approaches the periodisation of the Bronze Age in East Asia, there now seems little question that metallurgy spread from west to east across the steppes and neighbouring regions of Inner Eurasia (Chernykh 1992; Linduff & Mei 2009; Li & Chen 2012). The societies of the central plains of the Yellow River basin adopted bronze from that corridor zone but changed the steppe tradition in significant ways (Rawson 2017). While the Shang dynasty developed its distinctive bronze culture in the second millennium BC, the bronze-working traditions of the northern steppe continued to spread east, influencing Korea and Japan. Despite some relatively small typological differences, many bronze swords and spearheads found in the Korean peninsula and the Japanese islands share close similarities across a very wide area of northern Eurasia (cf. Kobayashi 2014; Matsumoto 2021). From mainland centres in southern China and Vietnam, bronze spread into Island Southeast Asia, most dramatically in the shape of Dong Son drums which reached as far south as Papua and Timor (Oliveira, O'Connor & Bellwood 2019). Dating of these drums, which may have been reused for long periods, is often insecure but they were still in use in the first millennium AD.

A major difference between the Bronze Ages of west and east Eurasia relates to the original relationship between centre and periphery. In the west, urban centres in the Near East expanded their connections with the European 'periphery' in their search for raw materials, transforming the societies of both regions. In eastern Eurasia, bronze was first introduced via the Inner Eurasian 'periphery' and then adopted – and often reinterpreted – by the 'core' states of the central plains (Rawson 2017). Island East Asia – the string of islands off the east coast of the mainland from Sakhalin down to Taiwan – seems to have followed a similar pattern of bronzisation, being first influenced by the Inner Eurasian periphery through Korea and only later by the Chinese core. This historical structure means that Island East Asia is an important region for understanding Bronze Age dynamics in eastern Eurasia.

2 Trade, Transculture and Maritime Connectivities

The Imazu site in Aomori, northern Japan has produced a three-legged jar from a Final Jōmon layer. The top of the vessel is damaged but it has a remaining height of only 11.4 cm. The jar has cord marking and red paint and belongs to the Ōbora C_2 type of the Final phase Kamegaoka culture (Shintani & Okada 1986) (Figure 3). Radiocarbon dates on charred material from other Ōbora C_2 sherds at Imazu have returned results of 1430–1396 and 1419–1383 cal BC, though a marine reservoir effect may make these dates a few centuries older than their absolute age (Horiuchi et al. 2015).

Tripods of the same shape as the Imazu jar are found in northern China after about 2500 BC (Wagner & Tarasov 2014). A variety of tripod forms are known from ancient China, but the more functional tripods served to boil water to steam cereals. The miniature size of the Imazu vessel rules out such a function. Tripods were rarely found in the Korean Bronze Age (Nelson 1999: 161) and An (1991) regards the Imazu tripod as a direct imitation of a Chinese vessel. Three more tripods from the same period found at other sites in Aomori may similarly have been influenced by continental Bronze Age contacts (Hudson et al. 2021). A possible connection with long-distance trade is suggested by salt-making pottery found at Imazu. Kamegaoka-style pottery sherds have

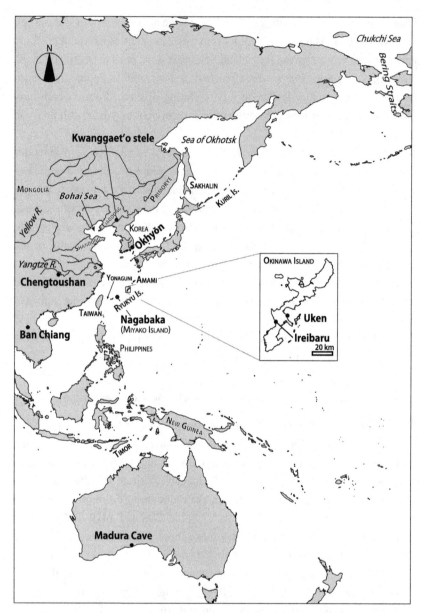

Figure 1 Eastern Eurasia and Australia with sites mentioned in the text. For sites in Japan, see Figure 2. Map drawn by J. Uchiyama.

been discovered from as far south as Okinawa, more than 2,000 km from the northern Tohoku heartland of the culture (Shitara 2018). The Ireibaru site on Okinawa (Figure 1) has also produced jade from Niigata in a Final Jōmon context.

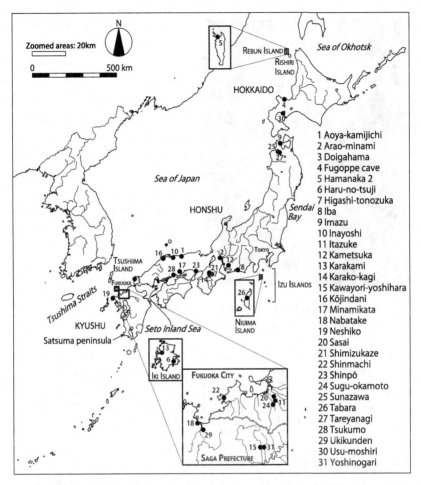

Figure 2 The Japanese islands with sites mentioned in the text.
Map drawn by J. Uchiyama.

The Kamegaoka people were participating in exchange networks over very long distances and with very different cultures. Many archaeologists have, however, assumed that it was only with the arrival of rice in southwest Japan that the Jōmon was opened to the outside and began to change. We might call this the 'Sleeping Beauty' model of the Jōmon world. Shitara (2014b: 8) imagines the reaction of Jōmon villagers in northern Honshu upon hearing about rice and other crops being grown in the west of the archipelago:

> [A] number of young people assembled a crew for a boat and packed it with trade goods such as masterpieces of pottery, red lacquered with intricate designs. Rowing against the current on rough seas they headed west.

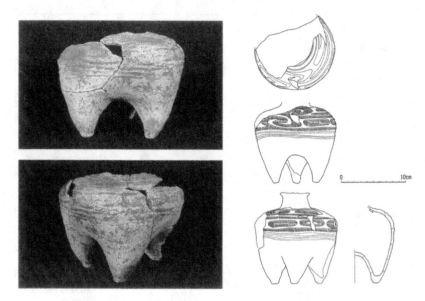

Figure 3 Final Jōmon tripod from the Imazu site.
Courtesy of Aomori Prefecture Archaeology Research Centre

The place they eventually reached was a settlement called Sasai on the plain of . . . Fukuoka. It was their first time to visit that place and the scene they saw was of rice paddy fields built by tall outsiders who were working in a friendly fashion with local people who – to judge from their faces – were their own comrades.

Shitara's story takes it as a given that the Jōmon people from the far north were country 'bumpkins' who had their eyes suddenly opened to civilisation by seeing and, later in the story, tasting rice. These were, however, the same Kamegaoka people who were imitating pottery from the Chinese mainland rather than just from the Korean peninsula, even if their knowledge of 'Chinese' pottery may have been obtained second-hand. Presumably they already knew all about about rice – even if they had decided not to grow it themselves. In total contrast to traditional 'rice-centred' views of Japanese history, it is such complex processes of reception and resistance which can be said to characterise bronzisation.

In many parts of Northeast Asia, millet farming initially spread overland within Neolithic cultural contexts, reaching Korea and the Primorye by the fourth millennium BC (Li et al. 2020). Around the same time, millet farmers in the Yellow River basin began to take up rice and many sites of the Yangshao culture have evidence for both millet and rice cultivation (Stevens & Fuller 2017). In the middle Yangtze, millet was adopted by some rice-farming societies, as for example at Chengtoushan (Nasu et al. 2012). In the Bronze Age, however, agricultural expansions changed completely with the addition of a maritime component.

Across Eurasia, the Bronze Age saw dynamic changes in food and farming. West Asian crops such as wheat and barley spread to East Asia while eastern millets spread west through Central Asia (Spengler 2019). As well as cereals, other plants such as cannabis spread along the new trans-Eurasian networks (Long et al. 2017; Ren et al. 2021). This Bronze Age 'food globalisation' often involved a fundamental reorganisation of agriculture through multicropping and longer use of the farming year (Liu et al. 2019). From the second millennium BC, the new crops began to spread to Korea and Japan. While broomcorn and foxtail millet had been grown in Korea since the fourth millennium BC, it was only through the *combination* of the five cereals (the two millets, rice, barley and wheat) that full-scale agriculture eventually reached the Japanese archipelago in the first millennium BC – much later than almost everywhere else in temperate Eurasia.

Notwithstanding critiques such as Jaffe and Flad (2018), the concept of 'food globalisation' provides some useful perspectives on economic trends in Bronze Age Eurasia. Nevertheless there were important discontinuities across the continent. Sherratt's (1981) concept of the 'secondary products revolution' proposed that from the Chalcolithic and Early Bronze Ages, domestic animals began to be exploited for milk, wool and traction. We now know that these innovations did not all develop at the same time, but by the later Bronze Age a combination of milking, wool production and animal traction for ploughing, transport and warfare were key elements in a new economic system, enabling expansion into previously marginal environments (Greenfield 2010). In East Asia, secondary products were adopted in a much more variable fashion, often influenced by regional differences in political control (Brunson et al. 2016). While inland areas such as Mongolia began to utilise milking around 3000 BC (Wilkin et al. 2020) and animal traction by the end of the second millennium BC (Taylor et al. 2015), in Island East Asia the process was much slower. In Japan, for example, horses were not introduced until the late fourth century AD (Sasaki 2018).

2.1 Express Trains and Slow Boats: The Sea and Bronze Age Farming Dispersals

The role of maritime voyaging in farming dispersals has been much discussed in Southeast Asian archaeology. Similar expansions also occurred in Northeast Asia, beginning in the Neolithic but taking off in the Bronze Age. Even if all of the populations involved did not possess bronze in the early stages, it makes sense to consider these movements as part of a broad trend towards new Bronze Age connectivities.

Recent research suggests that both inland _and_ maritime dispersals were important in the spread of rice and millets to southern China and mainland Southeast Asia (Zhang & Hung 2010; Stevens & Fuller 2017; Higham 2019). Rice and both foxtail and broomcorn millet were found in Taiwan by the third millennium BC (Qin & Fuller 2019). Farming populations then crossed from Taiwan to the northern Philippines around 2200 BC. In Island Southeast Asia, rice and millets were abandoned in favour of local crops such as bananas, breadfruit, taro and yams, but the Austronesian peoples nevertheless began a huge maritime dispersal which eventually took them and their changing food production systems across the Pacific as far as Hawai'i and Easter Island as well as west to Madagascar (Bulbeck 2008; Bellwood 2013; Spriggs 2018). Inland Inner Eurasia was the primary route for the continental east–west dispersal of cereals in the Late Neolithic and Bronze Ages (Spengler 2019). The suggestion that wheat may have spread to China via a maritime route has less support (Long et al. 2018). In Northeast Asia, there was a massive seaborne migration of farmers from Korea to the Japanese islands, a migration which began in the first millennium BC but continued until at least AD 700. As a result of this population movement, the modern Japanese retain only about 10 per cent hunter-gatherer (Jōmon) ancestry (Kanzawa-Kiriyama et al. 2017; Robbeets et al. 2021; Wang et al. 2021), a lower proportion than in many European countries (cf. Haak et al. 2015).

If maritime farming dispersals were thus a key motif in Bronze Age – or Bronze Age equivalent – societies in/from East Asia, the _speed_ of those dispersals varied enormously. Agriculture reached Korea a little earlier than Taiwan. From the end of the third millennium BC, the movement of farmers from Taiwan quickly gathered pace and by around 900 BC Austronesian populations had reached Tonga and Samoa. After a long pause, the settlement of the islands of eastern Polynesia then occurred around AD 1000 (Bellwood 2013: 196). From Easter Island to Madagascar, Austronesian migrations covered a distance of some 22,000 km (Bellwood 2013: 199). While noting the problem of different interpretations of the migratory pause in western Polynesia, Diamond (1988) has called this the 'express train' model. In Northeast Asia, maritime farming dispersals also alternated between phases of expansion and stasis but the overall tempo was much slower. Though present in southern Korea by 3500 BC, farming did not cross the 200 km-wide Tsushima straits to Japan until after 1000 BC. Several centuries of both maritime and inland agricultural dispersals in the main islands of Japan then followed (de Boer et al. 2020). The Ryukyu islands between Kyushu and Taiwan, however, were not settled by farmers until around AD 1000 (Takamiya et al. 2016) – roughly the same time when Polynesians were voyaging to Hawai'i, Easter Island and New Zealand. The southern Ryukyu islands – only just over 100 km north of Taiwan – were thus first occupied by farmers at around the same date as eastern Polynesia.

The maritime dispersal of farmers raises important theoretical questions in East Asian archaeology. Qin and Fuller (2019) argue that, in contrast to millet farmers, early wet-rice cultivators absorbed population growth through *in situ* intensification of production rather than by geographical expansion. They propose that rice farmers of the lower Yangtze exploited inland wetlands but engaged in little maritime activity. These arguments are surprising because many earlier researchers placed great emphasis on the maritime dispersal of rice. Japanese folklorist Kunio Yanagita (1875–1962) even developed a whole 'Ocean Road' theory to explain the spread of rice to Japan, though this is now discredited by archaeological research (Takamiya 2001). Qin and Fuller's interpretation may be reasonable for the lower Yangtze because that area already possessed extensive areas of coastal wetlands during the Neolithic. South of the Yangtze, a shortage of suitable wetlands may have delayed the spread of wet-rice farming and encouraged seafaring from around 3000 BC (Rolett et al. 2011). By contrast, in the Bronze Age, and especially after 1000 BC, the growth of deltaic and coastal plains in southern China and mainland Southeast Asia permitted a major expansion of rice farmers (Ma et al. 2020).

Rice began to spread north of the Yangtze from at least 4000 BC (Stevens & Fuller 2017). Most Neolithic rice from northern China comes from inland locations, suggesting rain-fed agriculture. In the Late Neolithic Longshan culture after 2600 BC, rice is found at several sites on the Shandong peninsula (Crawford et al. 2005; d'Alpoim Guedes 2015). From Shandong, rice is thought to have spread around the Bohai Sea to Liaodong and on to Korea by the late second millennium BC (Ahn 2010; Miyamoto 2019). Although there is little or no evidence for wet-rice farming in north-eastern Chinese sites at this time, in Korea, wet-rice paddy fields are known at several Bronze Age sites, including Okhyŏn, where a series of fields had a surface area of 2–3 m^2 each (Ahn 2010; Lee 2017). A few centuries later, rice reached Japan, where paddy fields are known from the Initial Yayoi phase (Mizoguchi 2013: 89–92). Not all agriculture in Bronze Age Japan relied on wet rice; many so-called dry fields for cultivating millets and other crops have also been found. Yet there is no question that a maritime component was involved in the spread of rice. The Japanese archipelago is perhaps the only place in the world where wet-rice agriculture spread by sea as a fully integrated system with all of its elements clearly in place from the beginning.

The relationship between maritime and land farming dispersals in Bronze Age Japan is nevertheless complex. As mentioned already, it has been argued that fishing was a minor activity in Yayoi farming villages. Carp aquaculture, known in China as early as eight thousand years ago, was also found in Yayoi Japan, having presumably diffused with rice farming (Nakajima et al. 2019). At the same time, there is evidence for specialised marine activities. In Hokkaido, there was an emphasis on large benthic fish, especially Pleuronectinae and bastard halibut (*Paralichthys olivaceus*), as well as swordfish (Takase 2019). Abalone became a common trade item down the Sea of Japan and it has been suggested that fishing groups from Kyushu made summer voyages up to Rebun island to catch abalone (see Hudson 2021a, *in press*). Tropical shells from Okinawa were traded with Kyushu but also carried as far north as Usu-moshiri in southern Hokkaido. The Bronze Age saw a major expansion in salt production in Europe and East Asia (Flad et al. 2005; von Falkenhausen 2006; Harding 2021) and Japan was no exception to that trend. During the second and first millennia BC, salt was made by boiling seawater in special pots along the Pacific coast of Honshu north of modern Tokyo. After cereal farming was introduced into western Japan, this Jōmon salt-making tradition became limited to the area around Sendai Bay until a new focus of production appeared in the Seto Inland Sea after 400 BC (Kawashima 2015).

Two important sites for understanding the relationship between maritime activity and farming dispersals in Bronze Age Japan are located in Aomori prefecture, the same region which produced the tripods discussed earlier in this Element. Both sites have remains of rice paddy fields: the Sunazawa paddies date back to the early fourth century BC, with Tareyanagi being slightly later (Aomori 1985; Hirosaki 1999). Both of these sites are located at a latitude of about 40° N, making them the most northerly prehistoric paddy fields from anywhere in the world. In the 1980s, it was proposed that rice farmers from Kyushu had 'leapfrogged' by boat up the Sea of Japan to establish the communities at Sunazawa and Tareyanagi (cf. Hudson 1990). New research has questioned this interpretation. It has been suggested that the Early Yayoi Ongagawa–style pottery found in northern Honshu was only 'imitating' that found in Kyushu (Takase 2017), an interpretation consistent with the concept of bronzisation. Since the artefacts excavated at Sunazawa do not include the stone or wooden agricultural tools found in western Japan, Fujio (2015, 2021) has proposed that local hunter-gatherers began paddy rice agriculture without the involvement of rice farmers from the outside. Given the difficulties in transfer-ring the complicated technology of rice paddy fields without personal experi-ence, this seems unlikely.[2] Segawa (2017: 80–1) notes that the early rice

---

[2] While conducting an ethnographic field school in the Akka district of Iwate prefecture, northern Honshu some twenty years ago, I had the opportunity to hear the experiences of the only family in the village who had tried to grow rice in the small mountain community. In the 1970s, at the height

cultivation at Sunazawa was established at about the same time as the abalone processing site at Hamanaka 2 on Rebun island, and suggests that the two developments may have been connected.

The relationship between societies of the sea and the land in Bronze Age Japan thus remains unclear in many respects. In part, this is due to the long-standing Confucian emphasis on rice farming as the hallowed pillar of Japanese civilisation, a bias which has marginalised the peoples of the sea. There is a large literature about the formation of 'mountain' or 'fishing' villages during the Yayoi period, but those communities are defined by their *lack* of rice cultivation, a condition which supposedly forced them to obtain rice through relations of social dependence with farming villages. Such views derive more from assumptions based on modern folklore or the history of the early modern Tokugawa era (1600–1868) than on evidence-based analyses of the Yayoi.

Some of the clearest evidence for maritime activity in the Yayoi comes from islands in the Tsushima straits between Korea and Japan. In its description of Tsushima and Iki, the *Wei zhi* noted the islanders 'travel by boat to buy grain in markets to the north and south' (Kidder 2007: 12). Sites on Iki island such as Karakami and Haru-no-tsuji have produced a rich, 'international' material culture including Chinese coins, Lelang pottery from the Han dynasty commandery in northern Korea, a three-winged bronze arrowhead (probably a crossbow bolt) (Figure 4) and even bones from Japan's earliest domesticated cat (Seyock 2003; Takesue 2009).[3] Haru-no-tsuji also has Japan's oldest known harbour. Trading connections between Kyushu and Korea at this time are clear from Yayoi pottery and Chinese coins – presumably used in exchange – found at Nŭkto on the south-east coast of Korea dating from the fourth century BC to the first century AD (Choy & Richards 2009).

Recent research has shown that standardised weights and measures were already in use in Yayoi Japan from at least the fourth century BC (Morimoto 2012; Fujio 2015). Yayoi balance weights seem to be most common at proto-urban sites in the Osaka–Kyoto region such as Kamei and Ikegami-sone, but are also known from Haru-no-tsuji. These weights are made of stone and are mostly rectangular in shape. Without suggesting a direct connection, the Yayoi weights are very similar in form to those from the Bronze Age Mediterranean (compare Hayama 2020: 85 with Ialongo 2018: 111). Balance weights, which are known from the third

---

of Japan's post-war economic boom, the male head of the family decided that their inability to grow their own rice was an embarrassing stigma and, with considerable difficulty, he set up a small area of paddy fields in the narrow valley. The family's struggles were not helped by the fact that the father was killed in a tragic accident a few years later.

[3] Domesticated cats are otherwise unknown in Japan until the ninth and tenth centuries AD (Hudson 2019: 33). Given that a wild leopard cat (*Prionailurus bengalensis euptilurus*) still exists on neighbouring Tsushima island, this find may require further confirmation.

Figure 4 Three-winged bronze arrowhead from Haru-no-tsuji, Iki island. This arrowhead is thought to have been used with a crossbow. Remaining size: length 2.8 cm, maximum width 1.1 cm, height 1.1 cm. Photo courtesy of Iki City Board of Education

millennium BC in the Near East and eastern Mediterranean, imply the shared quantification of economic value over wide areas (Ialongo 2018; Rahmstorf 2019).

A further facet of trade in Yayoi society relates to new findings of inkstones which suggest that writing was already in use in Bronze Age Japan, centuries earlier than previously thought. Several examples of imported Chinese artefacts with writing – including coins, bronze mirrors and the gold seal given by the Han emperor to the king of Na in Kyushu – are known from the first century AD.[4] Later, the Japanese started to copy inscriptions on mirrors, but it is sometimes argued that these attempts were primarily decorative (cf. Seeley 1991: 12–13). By contrast, the 'earliest texts of Japanese origin which show a clear understanding of the function of writing as a visual linguistic record' are said to date from the fifth century AD (Seeley 1991: 16). New research on inkstones appears to change this understanding completely. Flat stone inkstones similar to Han Chinese prototypes and sometimes with traces of black or red ink have been reported from more than 170 Yayoi and Kofun sites, with the earliest examples dating back to the second century BC (Yanagita 2020). Although there are around ten Late Yayoi–Early Kofun pots with inscribed Chinese characters, other written texts are not known from the Yayoi period. Takeo Kusumi (personal communication) suggests that cloth or wood may have been used for Yayoi documents, perhaps borrowing a similar technology to that used for the silk manuscripts found at the famous Former Han tomb of Mawangdui.

Historian Yoshihiko Amino (2012) showed that 'farmers' in premodern Japan sometimes also engaged in specialised long-distance shipping and commerce. Amino's research focussed on the medieval and early modern periods;

---

[4] See Fogel (2013) for a detailed analysis of this seal, including theories that it may be a forgery.

the social relations structuring maritime communities in the Bronze Age might have been quite different again, but there is a need to think about how farming articulated with other economic activities. The common narrative that wet-rice agriculture was the single hallowed path to Japanese culture is clearly false. Across Island East Asia, trade required boats, which needed large investments in time and money. Amino (2012: 13–16) has discussed how wealthy merchants of the early modern Tokugawa period financed large boats to trade up the Sea of Japan. These merchants did not own land or produce taxable crops. Despite their wealth, in the agrarian-centred class system of the Tokugawa they were called by derogatory terms such as *atamafuri* ('head shakers') or *mizunomi* ('water drinkers'). In Bronze Age Japan, if chiefs wanted bronze, they needed boats, and the relationship between agrarian and maritime economies was probably more favourable for those who could finance boatbuilding and trade. Using Bronze Age and Viking examples from Scandinavia, Ling and colleagues (2018) posit a 'maritime mode of production' as a way of modelling decentralised maritime confederacies based on raiding and trading as well as agropastoralism. It seems to me that this model might also be appropriate for understanding Bronze Age Japan. Some years ago, Ledyard (1975) used the term 'thalassocracy of Wa' to refer to early Japan. Although, to my knowledge, Ledyard never developed this proposal in detail, it shares a similar outlook with the 'maritime mode of production' and with work by Seyock (2003, 2004) and Takesue (2009) on maritime links across the Tsushima straits.

2.2 Boats and Maritime Technology

The Bronze Age saw a revolution in maritime technology. In the Mediterranean, long-distance voyaging began at first using canoes but with sailing ships growing in importance (Broodbank 2011: 31). A similar increase in voyaging is known in East Asia from the same time period. In the waters around Japan, there is clear evidence that many small islands such as those in the Okinawa archipelago, the Kurils and Rebun and Rishiri were visited more frequently during the Late Jōmon phase (*c*.2500–1250 BC) (Fitzhugh et al. 2016; Takamiya et al. 2016; Hudson et al. 2021). The Izu islands south of Tokyo may have been one exception to this trend; according to Oda (1990), sites there are most common circa six thousand to five thousand years ago, whereas the Late–Final Jōmon saw a decline in site numbers. This trend is confirmed by more recent research despite the discovery of a Late Jōmon ritual stone pavement at Tabara on Niijima island, a site which I helped excavate in the late 1980s. By the middle of the first millennium BC, however, people of the Yayoi culture were once again voyaging to and settling in the Izu islands (Sugiyama 2014).

The increase in marine voyaging around Japan from the Late Jōmon may reflect more patchy access to resources, in turn encouraging riskier, prestige-oriented trading and raiding (cf. Fitzhugh & Kennett 2010). One of the riskiest marine activities at this time was shark hunting. A Final Jōmon pot from Yamano-kami (Nagano) with an incised drawing of a hammerhead shark may be the oldest depiction of a shark from anywhere in the world (White et al. 2021). Shark teeth are common in many sites in the Japanese archipelago and southern Korea at this time. Nagabaka on Miyako island (Okinawa) has produced thirty-nine shark teeth, many with artificial perforations, dating from the second millennium BC to the early first millennium AD (Figure 5). Most of these teeth from Nagabaka are from tiger sharks (*Galeocerdo cuvier*). The potential dangers associated with shark hunting are demonstrated by an unusual find from Tsukumo shell midden (Okayama). Skeleton No. 24 from the Tsukumo cemetery is missing his right leg and left hand and has at least 790 perimortem traumatic lesions characteristic of a shark attack (White et al. 2021). The skeleton was radiocarbon dated to 1370–1010 cal BC.

In the Near East, sails first appear from the late fourth millennium BC and were widely used in the Bronze Age, although in Scandinavia, sails were not adopted until much later (Westerdahl 2015). There are a number of drawings of boats on Yayoi pottery and bronze bells. Most of these show oars and include

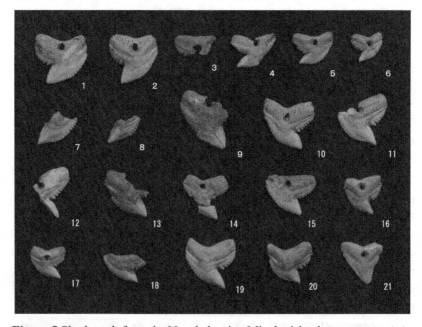

Figure 5 Shark teeth from the Nagabaka site, Miyako island. **Source:** Nagabaka Archaeology Project

quite large vessels, with between four and as many as eighty-one rowers, although the fact that boats with large numbers of oars – such as the central boat from Arao-minami (Figure 6) – often have unequal numbers on the two sides may suggest the intention was simply to draw a large vessel. The smaller boats at each end of the central vessel on the Arao-minami drawing are usually reconstructed as having sails (Habu 2010: 166). Although Woo (2018: 191–3) employs incised drawings of boats on tomb figurines (*haniwa*) from the Higashi-tonozuka tumulus (Nara) to argue *against* the use of sails at this time, those drawings show boats with oars but with a central post with 'banners' flowing in the wind. It is hard to say definitively that the Higashi-tonozuka drawings represent sails rather than banners; yet the action of the wind is clearly shown and it is plausible that these pictures were drawn to represent sails on the high seas. Cotton began to be used for sails in Japan from the fifteenth century (Nagahara & Yamamura 1988: 93–4). Prior to that, hemp, flax and woven grass mats were presumably used, unlike in Europe where wool was probably used for sails from the Bronze Age. In Hokkaido, twined grass mats were still used for sails by the Ainu in the early modern period (Tezuka 1998).

Boats also played an important role in the symbolic world of Bronze Age Japan. A pot from Inayoshi (Tottori) depicts a small boat with four or five rowers wearing elaborate feather-like headdresses and a sun circle positioned above (Figure 7). Similar ship and sun motifs are known from rock art in Fugoppe cave (Hokkaido), perhaps dating to around the first century AD, and from Mezurashikuzuka, Gorōyama and other Kofun tombs in Kyushu (Zancan 2013; Hudson 2021a). Ships with warriors wearing feather headdresses are also known from Dong Son bronzes in Southeast Asia (Oliveira et al. 2019). In the Near East and Europe, representations of ships and the sun, sometimes with horses or birds in association, have been analysed as part of a widely shared mythology relating to the journey of the sun from night into day (Kristiansen & Larsson 2005). It is unclear if similar ideas spread to East Asia, or if the Yayoi and Dong Son representations are pure coincidence.

2.3 Trade and the Bronze Economy

Notwithstanding recent advances in research, many aspects of the metal trade in Bronze Age East Asia remain poorly understood. We still don't know enough about sources of tin, copper and lead in the region. Africa has even been suggested as a source for Shang bronzes with highly radiogenic lead isotopes (Sun et al. 2016). Though this African proposal has been critiqued (Liu et al. 2018), the source of the radiogenic lead used in Shang bronzes remains unknown. However, several ore sources across China were exploited in the

Figure 6 Drawing of boats from the Arao-minami site. Courtesy of Gifu Prefecture Cultural Properties Preservation Centre

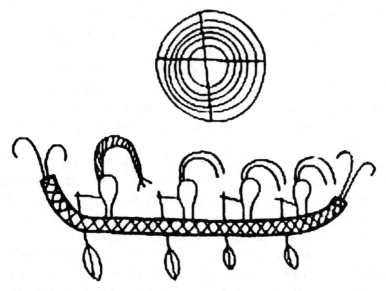

Figure 7 A Yayoi boat pictured on pottery from Inayoshi (Tottori). The illustration here shows the reconstruction by Harunari (1991). Kidder (2007: 43) has an alternative reconstruction with five rowers. **Source:** redrawn by J. Uchiyama from Hudson (1992)

Bronze Age and the overall picture appears to be one of exchange between multiple regional centres (Chen et al. 2016).

Japan has large deposits of many metals including copper, iron, silver and gold. In later times, these deposits were extensively exploited. At the end of the sixteenth century, Japan is said to have been producing one-third of the world's silver (Nagahara & Yamamura 1988: 82). Fluctuations in Japanese silver exports to China have even been proposed as a factor leading to the fall of the Ming dynasty (Atwell 2005). The *Shoku Nihongi*, a text completed in AD 797, records the joy of the central court upon receiving copper mined in Musashi province near modern Tokyo in 708. An imperial edict announced, 'It is Our opinion that this is a Treasure made manifest because the Gods that dwell in Heaven and the Gods that dwell on Earth have deigned to enrich and bless us' (Sansom 1924: 17). The name of the reign–era was immediately changed to Wadō ('Japanese copper'), tax exemptions were announced for Musashi, certain (unspecified) criminals were given an amnesty and rewards were bestowed 'upon aged people and persons who have displayed the virtues of filial piety or connubial faithfulness' (Sansom 1924: 17). While Musashi was nominally under the control of the Yamato kingdom, it is interesting to note the generous measures employed to secure its support. Some four decades later, a large gold mine in Mutsu province in north-east Honshu was also being exploited and Japan became a major source of gold for China, where deposits of that metal were relatively rare (von Verschuer 2006: 65–6). Iron production began in several regions of the archipelago in the sixth century AD (Matsugi 2018). During the Bronze Age, however, Japan and the rest of Island East Asia did not produce raw materials for metal production and all bronze was imported, although by the second century BC some weapons were being cast in Kyushu using imported bronze (Iwanaga 2018).

Compared to many parts of Europe and the central plains of China, bronze tools and weapons were rare in Yayoi Japan (Sahara 1987a: 282). How did people in the Japanese islands pay for bronze imports? What was traded instead? Using textual sources and inscriptions, Nanba (2016) calculated that around the time of the Former Han emperor Wu (reigned 141–87 BC), a kilogramme of bronze was exchanged within China for around three hundred *wuzhu* coins. This was the equivalent of 150 litres of unhulled grain. A slave, by contrast, cost the equivalent of 50–60 kg of bronze. Though no direct evidence exists, Japanese archaeologists assume that the price of bronze carried to Japan could have been ten or more times higher than in China (Nanba 2016; Kitajima 2019: 153). As possible goods carried from Japan in exchange for bronze, suggestions have included cereals, cloth, marine products, lumber and slaves. The high price of slaves in China suggests that captives from the Japanese islands would have been highly sought after. The *Hou Han shu* records that a king in Japan sent 160 slaves (*shengkou*) to the Han emperor in the second century AD (Kidder 2007: 26).[5] Given that the agricultural economy was more productive in China, cereals are perhaps an unlikely trade item though they cannot be ruled out; few premodern states would turn down extra grain when available. Textile production was also more advanced on the continent but various brocades, dyed cloth and animal furs were given as diplomatic gifts by the Yamato court from at least the seventh century (Aston 1972). Amber and agate are also mentioned in the *Nihon shoki* (AD 720) as royal gifts. Timber is known to have been traded to China by the thirteenth century (von Verschuer 2006: 69–70) and probably has a longer history. Marine products such as abalone may have been exchanged at an early stage. Okinawa has been suggested as a source for the cowrie shells found in many Bronze Age sites in China but recent studies have concluded that the cowrie species found in Chinese sites were not common in the Ryukyus (Pearson 2013: 127).

---

[5] For a discussion of earlier debates in Japanese historiography over the term *shengkou*, see Young (1958: 154–61).

The ancient Chinese were further interested in Japan as a mysterious land of immortality. An alchemist named Xu Fu, sent by the First Emperor of the Qin dynasty (221–207 BC) to find this country, had initially returned to China empty-handed, whereupon he made up a story about a Sea God leading him to a place where an official with a bronze face and a dragon body showed him a palace with the plants of longevity. Access to that palace would require extra gifts of 'young boys, virgins, and craftsmen of every kind'. According to the story, Xu Fu's wish was granted and he returned with the gifts but then stayed in Japan (Wang 2005: 8). Chinese literati also saw Japan as a mystical land located near the source of the sun. The Tang writer Xu Ning sent off a Japanese envoy with a poem, the beginning of which is paraphrased by Schafer (1989: 393) as 'Your homeland is at the limit of the world we know, Beyond even Fu-sang, the land of the sun. Thence you came to the seat of *our* glorious Sun.'

Despite the high value of bronze in Yayoi Japan, it was often deposited in hoards. Yayoi hoards include bronze bells (*dōtaku*) and weapons. As in Europe, there is a large literature on the meaning of these hoards. Bells are often assumed to have been linked with rituals related to rice cultivation and to have served to cement communal solidarity (see Hudson 1992: 153–5 for a discussion of some classic theories). By contrast, Kuwabara (1995) argued that hoards were a way of making bronze scarce to increase the political status of elites. The ethnologist Ōbayashi (1975) speculated that hoards were connected to the worship of weapons, a custom which he believed had entered Japan from the northern steppes. A further possible explanation for weapon hoards might be related to warrior sociality. If Bronze Age warriors can be assumed to have negotiated liminal positions with respect to their communities (Ling & Cornell 2017), a further possible explanation for weapon hoards might be related to the shedding of warrior identity – whether temporarily or otherwise – through what Anderson (2018: 223) calls 'post-conflict cleaning rituals'. The placement of Yayoi bronze hoards on hillsides outside agricultural communities may support this idea. Non-utilitarian weapons may have been used in hoards to symbolise a 'post-conflict' status. The fact that most warriors seem to have been buried in cemeteries in their own towns or villages suggests means of sociality whereby warriors could return to the community.

The largest bronze hoard known from Japan was found in the 1980s at Kōjindani (Shimane) and contained 358 swords, sixteen spearheads and six bells (Piggott 1989). These objects had been produced over several centuries and buried in the latter part of the Middle Yayoi (Shimane Board of Education 1996), a phase now usually dated to the last four centuries of the first millennium BC. Though smaller than some hoards found in Europe – four thousand bronze axes were found at Maure-de-Bretagne in north-west France, for example (Briard 1965) – Kōjindani is nevertheless much larger than other hoards from Japan. A decade later, another hoard of thirty-nine bronze bells was found at Kamo-iwakura, three kilometres from Kōjindani (Torrance 2016). The Kōjindani hoard is situated in the old province of Izumo on the Sea of Japan coast, a region known both for close connections with the Korean peninsula and for its political role in the Bronze Age archipelago (de Boer et al. 2020). Wengrow (2011) has built on Childe to note that bronze hoards in Europe are often situated along routes of long-distance trade. In this reading, hoards are less about local communities and more related to transcultural connections. While many archaeologists have explored the role of local elites in hoard depositions in the Yayoi (e.g., Adachi 2011), the evidence from Izumo may also be consistent with Wengrow's interpretation. Wengrow (2011) goes on to make a distinction between 'sacrificial' and 'archival' economies. The presence of standardised weights and measures and inkstones in Bronze Age Japan shows that the economy had developed 'archival' elements. At the same time, there remained a 'sacrificial' side in bronze hoards as well as in the *Wei zhi* account of 'abstainers' used on voyages to China. On such missions, the text explains, 'there is always one man who does not comb his hair, does not remove the lice, lets his clothes become dirty, does not eat meat, and does not get near women'. If the journey is successful, he is given 'slaves and valuable things', but 'if disease or injuries occur', he is killed (Kidder 2007: 15). More research is needed, but given the different geographical distribution of hoards around the Seto Inland Sea summarised by Barnes (2015: 325–6), it is possible that 'archival' economies were initially common in Kyushu and the western Inland Sea whereas 'sacrificial' economies dominated the eastern Inland Sea.

2.4 Bronze Age Demographic Change in East Asia

The period from the end of the Neolithic to the Bronze Age saw major demographic changes in Europe. The fact that remarkably similar changes also occurred in East Asia suggests that the underlying causal mechanisms may have been common to many Eurasian societies at this time.

From the beginning of the Neolithic, more sedentary lifestyles had led to population growth as part of the 'Neolithic Demographic Transition' (Bocquet-Appel 2011). In East Asia, early sedentism was associated with pottery and, in northern areas, the widespread use of semi-subterranean pit houses. In many parts of Northeast Asia, sedentism developed *before* farming (Pearson 2006; Shelach-Lavi et al. 2019). As cereal farming became more important, the type of agriculture engaged in by Neolithic East Asian societies affected their demographic patterns. Wet-rice farmers, who had invested time and labour in elaborate paddy fields, tended to stay in one place, absorbing population growth through extra labour inputs. Millet farmers, by contrast, usually adopted a more dispersed or expansionary settlement pattern (Qin & Fuller 2019). Within millet farming societies in northern China, community structure was also influenced by different risk-buffering strategies resulting from environmental conditions (Drennan et al. 2020).

Neolithic population growth could be subject to fluctuations due to climate, disease, or the low resilience of early farming systems (Shennan et al. 2013; Stevens & Fuller 2012). During the transitional period from the Neolithic to the Bronze Age, one particular population crash known as the 'Late Neolithic decline' took place, which was found in several regions of Eurasia. Climate change, the immigration of steppe pastoralists and trade have been suggested as possible causes of this decline (Kristiansen 2015), but recent findings of plague (*Yersinia pestis*) from Sweden in an individual dated 5040–4867 BP (Rascovan et al. 2019) and in two individuals dated to 4556 and 4430 BP from Lake Baikal (Yu et al. 2020) show that there is also a need to reconsider the role of epidemic disease. The Neolithic had forced humans, plants and animals into new intimacies. Scott (2017) calls Neolithic villages 'multi-species resettlement camps' and has summarised the evidence for new zoonotic diseases and declining human health. The economic and social interactions of the Bronze Age brought Eurasian societies into ever closer contact, ideas and artistic styles spread with peoples and languages, and epidemic diseases such as plague began to spread further across Eurasia, 'piggybacking' on new trade networks.

In the Late Neolithic, a population crash occurred in parts of East Asia. In China, there was no overall decline but a complex, asynchronous pattern (Jaffe & Hein, 2021), which Hosner and colleagues (2016) speculate may reflect the impact of plague. In Korea, radiocarbon proxy data suggest a population drop around 4800 cal BP (Oh et al. 2017). In Japan, a population decline in the third millennium BC was first analysed by Koyama (1978), who concluded that population levels dropped almost 40 per cent across Kyushu, Shikoku and Honshu as a whole, and by almost 60 per cent in central Honshu. Later research, looking in more detail at particular regional sequences in Japan, has supported the trends identified by Koyama (Imamura 1996: 95–6; Hudson 1999: 140; Sekine 2014; Crema et al. 2016; Crema & Kobayashi 2020). Crema and Kobayashi (2020) date the start of the population crash in central Honshu to around 2900 BC. Epidemic disease was already suggested as a possible cause of the Late Neolithic decline in Japan by Oikawa and Koyama (1981) and Kidder (1995, 2007). Given the new biomolecular analyses of *Y. pestis*, there is a need for similar studies to explore the role of plague in Late Neolithic and Bronze Age East Asia.

Following the Late Neolithic decline, the Bronze Age itself saw a large population increase in Europe but an apparent decline in the Near East (Müller 2013). Bronze Age East Asia saw large population increases in China (Hosner et al. 2016), Korea (Oh et al. 2017) and Japan (Koyama 1978). Crops were moved beyond previous ecological boundaries and there was a significant expansion in arable land (Liu et al. 2019). Urbanisation developed, especially in northern China, where some cities may have housed up to half a million people by the first millennium BC (von Falkenhausen 2008).

2.5 Alaska, Australia and the Ryukyus: The Frontiers of the Eurasian Bronze Age

A focus on trade, connectivities and bronzisation raises the problem of the geographical frontiers of the Bronze Age world. Methodologically, this is a difficult question. On one hand, archaeologists have sometimes been overly keen to link distant peoples and places, often without proper evaluation of dating, yet at the same time there is no doubt that certain regions have been neglected in debates over ancient globalisations (Boivin & Frachetti 2018; Spriggs 2018). Bronzisation, it can be argued, began to impact the Japanese islands from as early as the third millennium BC (Hudson et al. 2021), but what were the geographical limits of that process? Here I briefly consider this question by examining Alaska, Australia and the Ryukyu islands.

As recently summarised by Dyakonov and colleagues (2019), bronze appears very early in Siberia, probably reaching the middle reaches of the Lena river by the end of the third millennium BC. By the early second millennium, there is evidence for bronze casting in Yakutia and a mould for casting bronze, dated circa 1000 BC, has been found some 50 km from the Chukchi Sea. Iron also appeared very early, with iron artefacts present in Yakutia by perhaps 800 BC and on the Sea of Okhotsk coast by at least the end of the first millennium BC. These metals seem to have spread across the northern forest zone, which, as noted by Uchiyama and colleagues (2020), is an underappreciated belt of connectivity across ancient Eurasia (Figure 8). Although metals reached eastern Siberia very early, there are only two bronze finds in Alaska, only one of which is dated (to around AD 1200) (Dyakonov et al. 2019). The Bering Straits thus seem to have formed the north-eastern frontier of the expanding world of the Eurasian Bronze Age, perhaps because there were no trade goods in Alaska which could not also be found in Siberia. In later centuries, iron was traded into Alaska and used for the ornate walrus ivory carving associated with the Old Bering Strait culture, which began around AD 300 but reached its peak flores-cence circa 650–1250 (Mason & Rasic 2019). Since the early work of Laufer

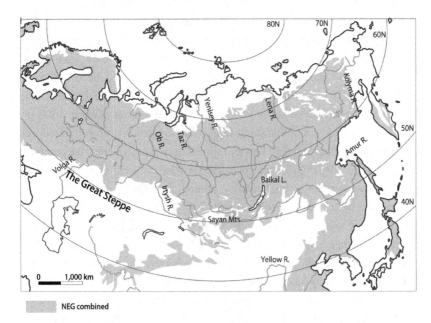

NEG combined

Figure 8 Forest zones of the north Eurasian greenbelt (NEG) with major rivers.
Source: drawn by J. Uchiyama

(1913), it has been suggested that trade in walrus ivory brought the Bering Straits into the Eurasian world system (Mason 2009); artefacts made of walrus ivory are also found in the Okhotsk culture of Hokkaido (*c*.AD 500–1200) and Kikuchi (2004: 117–25) makes a similar proposal for the Sea of Okhotsk region.

Moving south, in Island Southeast Asia, we can recognise two phases of heightened interaction with mainland Eurasia: the period between 2000 and 1000 BC saw the spread of Neolithic lifeways, while bronze and, to a lesser extent, iron reached the region from around 300 to 100 BC (Spriggs 2018), although the bronze axes from Gua Harimau in Sumatra may date from slightly earlier (Bellwood 2017: 313). The dispersal of Austronesian populations through Island Southeast Asia and beyond has sometimes been debated in terms of a stark choice between Neolithic farming versus maritime trade (Bulbeck 2008). Given the Bronze Age time frame of this dispersal, I find it more useful to think in terms of a *combination* of farming and trade.

Island Southeast Asia certainly experienced major social and economic changes at this time, but what about Australia? Did it remain totally isolated from the transformations of the Eurasian Bronze Age? Important changes in the archaeological record of Australia after around 2000 BC have, in fact, been recognised for some time. Population sizes seem to have grown after 2000 BC (Hiscock 2008). Backed artefacts (microliths) and edge-ground axes spread widely across many areas of Australia in the second and first millennia BC, reflecting new connectivities over the continent (Hiscock & Maloney 2017). Recent research shows the dingo was introduced at this time from Island Southeast Asia, although a New Guinea origin has also been suggested (Ardalan et al. 2012). A direct radiocarbon date on a dingo bone from Madura Cave on the southern Nullarbor Plain has produced a result of about 1300 BC (Figure 1). The authors of that study suggest the dingo was probably introduced to Australia quite soon before that and spread very rapidly across the continent (Balme et al. 2018). Evidence for offshore island visitation and settlement suggests increased maritime activity around Australia from the late third millennium BC (Bowdler 1995; Sim & Wallis 2008). Finally, the linguistic record seems to show a very widespread dispersal of Pama–Nyungan languages, probably beginning in the middle-to-late Holocene (Evans & Jones 1997; Bouckaert et al. 2018). Debate continues over biological evidence that a new population may have reached Australia at this time (Bellwood 2013: 119–21). While the precise context remains unclear, it remains a reasonable hypothesis that Bronze Age transformations in Eurasia and into Island Southeast Asia had some secondary or 'knock-on' impacts on Australia.

Both Alaska and Australia lay outside the Eurasian Bronze Age system, though were perhaps not totally isolated from that world. These cases are interesting but hardly surprising. Much more unexpected is the Bronze Age status of the Ryukyu islands. The Ryukyu archipelago stretches some 1,300 km between Kyushu and Taiwan. Geographically speaking, it can be considered central to Island East Asia, a position it certainly fulfilled during the medieval era when a trading state based on Okinawa island traded widely across East and Southeast Asia (Pearson 2013; Smits 2019). Yet during the period considered in this Element, the Ryukyus maintained a quite different historical trajectory. As far as we know, the southern Ryukyu islands from Yonaguni to Miyako remained totally isolated until the start of the second millennium AD. Although Yonaguni is only 110 km from Taiwan, and according to Kinoshita (2019a) the high mountains of Taiwan are visible from Yonaguni, neither rice or millets spread north from Taiwan, and the same is true of bronze, which was present on Taiwan by 400 BC (Hung & Chao 2016). Nephrite artefacts from Taiwan were widely distributed across Southeast Asia in the Bronze Age (Hung et al. 2007), but none have been found in the Ryukyus. The central and northern islands of the Ryukyu chain, by contrast, were in frequent contact with Japan. In the periodisation frequently employed by Okinawan archaeologists, the prehistoric 'Shell Mound period' is divided, around 600 BC, into Early and Late stages based on links with the Yayoi cultures of Kyushu. A long-distance trade in tropical shells developed at this time and, according to Kinoshita (2019a:

326), persisted until the seventh century AD. However, this trade network appears to have had little long-lasting impact on the societies of the Okinawa and Amami islands (Table 1).

Rice and other cereals are reasonable candidates for commodities exchanged to the Ryukyus from Kyushu. While many archaeologists have assumed that the shell trade would have led to the onset of agriculture in the Ryukyu islands, this was not the case. We have little concrete evidence for goods traded into Okinawa at this time, though cloth, silk and rice wine have been proposed as possibilities. Thanks to the work of archaeobotanist Hiroto Takamiya, the Okinawa and Amami islands have the best sequence of directly dated plant remains from anywhere in Japan. Takamiya's work has shown that wild plants such as nuts (*Casatanopsis sieboldii, Actinidia rufa, Machilus thunbergii*) and grape (*Vitis* sp.) were exclusively consumed until the end of the first

Table 1 Possible Bronze Age impacts on the Late Shell Mound culture of Okinawa and Amami. The left column is based on Kinoshita (2019b).

Archaeological features of the Late Shell Mound phase (Okinawa and Amami)	Connections with Yayoi Kyushu/ Bronze Age East Asia
Settlements move from terraces to coastal areas	Suggests new focus on the sea and maritime links
Stone tool assemblages little changed from previous phase	Implies few changes in subsistence and food processing
Ceramic decoration becomes plainer	Mirrors similar changes in western Japan since the Late Jōmon
Ceramic vessels become larger	Possibly reflects increased use of Scaridae and other large fish[1]
Imported Yayoi pottery	Dozens of vessels imported, primarily to Okinawa island (Shinzato 2018)
Metal artefacts	*Bronze*: mirror fragment; sword hilt fragment; arrowhead. *Iron*: fragments of axes and other tools; iron fishhook (from Tanegashima); Warring States knife-shaped coins (*mingdaoqian*)
Coral cist burials	Probable influence from stone cists in Kyushu

Note: [1] This interpretation is from Kinoshita (2019b), but it should be noted that the Late Neolithic cultures of the southern Ryukyus made extensive use of Scaridae (parrotfish) without possessing any pottery at all.

millennium AD. After that, a combination of cereals (foxtail millet, wheat, barley and rice) spread to Amami from the eighth century, to Okinawa from the tenth, and then to the previously isolated southern Ryukyus from the twelfth (Takamiya et al. 2016). Domesticated animals (pigs, cattle, horses, goats and chickens) spread south to the islands at the same time (Toizumi 2018). Historical linguists have argued that Ryukyuan, a sister language of Japanese, dispersed with farming (Pellard 2015).

The tropical shells brought to Kyushu in the Yayoi period were made into bracelets whose angular forms recall bronze and yet whose colour resembles white jade. These artefacts can be considered as examples of 'creative translation' from one medium to another (cf. Sofaer et al. 2013). Writing about Bronze Age China, Campbell (2020) notes that these materials would originally have been 'white, bright, and, or, lustrous – all qualities associated with the spirits in later texts'. In Japan, shell artefacts were later copied in bronze and there is even a wooden replica of a shell bracelet from Karako-kagi (Nara) (Pearson 1990: 919). Shell bracelets were traded from Okinawa to north-west Kyushu from the beginning of the Yayoi, centuries before bronze became common in the Japanese archaeological record (Nakazono 2011: 51). It is unclear whether shells were chosen as a replacement material because bronze was so expensive to obtain, especially in the first half of the Yayoi period. Alternatively, perhaps Okinawan shells mirrored or 'stood in' for bronze while originating from even more exotic sources and cycles of production. Of course, shell artefacts served – like bronze – to reinforce the status of Yayoi elites, but either way the Yayoi shell trade in my view presupposes some knowledge of bronze as a desirable material.

Yayoi pots were transported to Okinawa from Kyushu, mostly from the Satsuma peninsula (Nakazono 2011; Shinzato 2018). That Yayoi pottery in Okinawa had a certain value can be deduced from the fact that it was often repaired when cracked. The mainland Japanese, by contrast, were less interested in Okinawan products except for shells, and only one Okinawan pot has been found on Kyushu. This pot was reported at the Takahashi site on the Satsuma peninsula (Kagoshima), a settlement which Nakazono (2011) regards as a major shell trade entrepôt. Aside from pottery, only a handful of exotic objects reached Okinawa at this time. These include glass beads, spindle whorls, coins, fragments of iron axes, a piece of the hilt of a bronze sword, a fragment of a Han bronze mirror and Lelang pottery (Nakazono 2011). Three-winged bronze arrowheads of Han crossbow style have been found at Uken and Uza-no-hamayabaru on Okinawa (Ashiya Board of Education 2007). Many of these artefacts can be linked with the East Asian mainland, raising the possibility that they were imported directly rather than via Kyushu, although no ordinary Chinese or Korean ceramics have been excavated from these Okinawan sites.

In summary, it is very hard to situate the Ryukyus in the East Asian Bronze Age. On one hand, there was very developed maritime trade and voyaging but, on the other, there was little apparent desire by the Ryukyuans to participate in the Bronze Age world system. Kinoshita (2019b: 34) writes that for the Ryukyuans, 'neither cereals or the new materials [bronze] were attractive enough for them to become partial to' and she concludes that behind their reluctance to accept Yayoi culture were the stable resources of the coral reefs. To play on the title of Kristiansen and Larsson (2005), the Ryukyus at this time seem to be a case of travels *without* transformation.

3 Bronze and Warrior Aristocracies in the Japanese Islands

European archaeologists have proposed that 'the Bronze Age represents the *global* emergence of a militarized society with a martial culture materialized in a package of new, efficient weapons that remained in use for millennia to come' (Horn & Kristiansen 2018: 1, emphasis added). While this proposal makes sense for Europe and the Near East, to what extent can it also be applied to East Asia? In this section, I use the Japanese islands as a case study to explore this problem.

Until the 1980s, the Bronze Age Yayoi period in Japan was widely regarded as a 'peaceful, non-military, shamanistic and ceremonially religious' society (Egami 1964: 44). This was contrasted with the warlike 'Horseriders' of the following Kofun era under the assumption that violence and warfare were introduced to Japan from the outside. The discovery of sites such as Yoshinogari (Saga) changed this understanding and, over the past three decades, the Yayoi has come to be seen as the period marking the advent of full-scale warfare in the archipelago. At the same time, however, many scholars continue to emphasise the 'ritual' aspects of Yayoi society. Almost all Japanese books on the Yayoi structure their discussion of bronze around ritual rather than warfare. Yayoi specialist Shinichirō Fujio is not unusual in making the broader argument that Bronze Age Japan differed significantly from western Eurasia in terms of war and weapons: 'From the perspective of world history', he writes, 'in the West bronze was used for sharp weapons (arms) but in the East Asian world centred on China, it was used for ritual objects' (Fujio 2015: 110).[6] Such claims recall those of Chang (1983, 1989) who stressed the political role of ritual and shamanism in Bronze Age China. Yet there is little question that 'warfare was an integral and essential part of the religious system' in Bronze Age China (Yates 1999: 9; see also Yuan & Flad 2005; Campbell 2018;

---

[6] Fujio distinguishes between two types of ritual objects, which he calls *saiki* and *reiki*. Though not widely used in Yayoi archaeology, these terms appear to suggest a distinction between 'native' and 'Chinese' rituals.

Sanft 2020). How, then, should we characterise the relationships between violence, ritual and society in the Japanese archipelago?

3.1 The Violence of Rice

In my own earlier work, I have also been guilty of overemphasising the ritual aspects of Yayoi violence. In a 1992 essay on Yayoi ritual and religion – a paper which after some thirty years unfortunately remains the most detailed treatment of its topic in English – I discussed the so-called hunting design bronze mirror from Gunma prefecture, which is thought to date to the third century AD (illustrated and discussed in Hudson 1992: 147–50). This mirror has two concentric bands of decoration. In the inner band, four human figures are interspersed with deer; two of the figures carry shields (or possibly bows) and spears or halberds, one holds a jar aloft, while the fourth has its empty hands upraised. The outer band has ten figures, eight of whom are armed with shields and swords, one with a shield and spear/halberd, and one again stands with arms upraised. In my earlier essay, I followed Shitara's (1991) interpretation that this mirror depicts mock warfare as part of a seasonal round of agricultural rituals.

Deer are the most common animal depicted in Yayoi art (Figure 9). Though dating some five hundred years after the end of the Yayoi, the eighth-century *Harima fudoki* is frequently used to link deer with rice through the story of rice seeds germinating after being planted in the fresh blood of a deer (Palmer 2015). The deer on the Gunma mirror have different-sized antlers, and small circles located above the animals may represent the movement of the sun or moon, both features perhaps suggesting a seasonal round related to cultivation. Alternatively, deer can be seen as a symbol of the wild and thus the bravery and heroism required as part of the warrior ethos. The two figures with upraised arms would seem to be examples of *adorants* or 'persons performing an act of adoration or invocation to a higher being' (Maringer 1979: 215). Johannes Maringer, a German prehistorian who taught archaeology in Japan in the 1950s, noted that such adorants are common in prehistoric art around the world. This also helps us to understand the fact that the adorants on the Gunma mirror only have three fingers on each hand since the gesture of prayer adopted by the adorant is often depicted by an emphasis on outstretched fingers. Of the examples illustrated by Maringer (1979), an urn from the Caucasus has an adorant hunter with three fingers like the Gunma mirror. Another Yayoi example is an incised sherd from Shimizukaze (Nara) where the adorant has a drawing of a deer on its torso (Figure 10a).[7]

---

[7] A theriomorphic Middle Jōmon clay figurine from Misaka (Yamanashi) also has three fingers on its only preserved hand (Maringer 1974: 129).

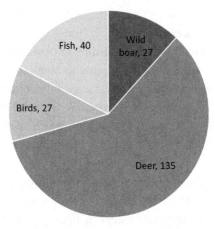

Figure 9 Numbers of the four most common animals represented on bronze bells from Yayoi Japan. Data from Shitara (2014b: 47–8)

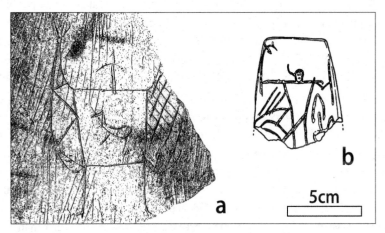

Figure 10 (a) Drawing on pottery from Shimizukaze (Nara). (b) Drawing on a ceramic bell-shaped object from Kawayori-yoshihara (Saga). Drawn by J. Uchiyama

Interpretation of the Gunma mirror – and indeed other Bronze Age art from Japan – is difficult, but in contrast to my earlier work, I would today be more inclined to approach it from the framework of violence rather than agricultural ceremonies. This distinction is not, of course, an absolute one; in the ancient world, violence and warfare always involved ritual aspects and it is difficult to separate the two (Campbell 2018; Fagan et al. 2020). Rituals were polyvalent. Armit (2020: 442) notes that ritual can be seen as a *formalisation* of important aspects of life. This formalisation is often enacted through performance: for instance, headhunting in Iron Age Europe could have been associated with a desire to ensure the fertility of crops and the community. In Bronze Age China, warfare was connected to both hunting and agriculture (Yates 1999: 14). From this perspective, the major problem with the Japanese literature is its insistence on trying to *separate* the ritual from the non-ritual aspects of Bronze Age violence, a separation which stems in part from the strong Marxist tradition in early post-war Japanese archaeology (cf. Kaner 2011).

Let us look briefly at two examples of the role of shamanism in framing Yayoi ritual and violence, one an artistic depiction and one an actual skeleton. Terasawa (2000: 104) interprets a human figure on a small ceramic bell-shaped object found at Kawayori-yoshihara (Saga), which probably dates to the first century BC, as a 'shaman'. The figure has what may be a feather headdress; a sword is carried at the waist and a shield and halberd are held in the hands (Figure 10b). To the right of the figure, an oval object is possibly a depiction of a bronze bell. To the left, three lines may represent arrows piercing an animal such as a deer or wild boar. In the second example, at Doigahama (Yamaguchi), a headless male skeleton had been shot with thirteen stone arrowheads. Two shark teeth found with the skeleton are also possible arrowheads. According to Matsushita (1994: 46), the presence of two *Sinustrombus latissimus* shell bracelets and the 'overkill' associated with his death identify this individual as a shaman. Matsushita's argument is that a ritual leader of the community was sacrificed by his own group members because of the transgressive danger he represented. In these and other examples, the possibility that 'shamanistic' figures were involved in warfare is not totally dismissed. Yet there is no more evidence to suggest the discoveries from Kawayori-yoshihara or Doigahama represent ritual specialists rather than professional warriors. Other finds of Yayoi skeletons subjected to 'overkill' include a male with seventeen arrowheads from the Shinpō site in Kobe; since this individual was buried in a row with two other males, Matsugi (2001: 30) argues all three were killed in combat at the same time.

As noted earlier in this Element, Japanese archaeologists have regarded the Yayoi as part of an East Asian Bronze Age culture centred on ritual objects and 'ritualised' weapons. Chang (1989) saw this as a different pattern from the ancient Near East where bronze was also used for tools of production. Rawson (2017) extends this approach by proposing three aspects of 'reception and resistance' to bronze technology in the central plains of the Yellow River. The first was that bronze was used primarily for vessels rather than weapons. Chinese bronze vessels were elaborate and could be extremely large. The heaviest surviving example weighs 875 kg – the largest bronze vessel cast anywhere in the ancient world (Shelach-Lavi 2015: 212). By weight, this vessel alone is equivalent to almost half of *all* bronze excavated from Yayoi Japan by the 1980s, according to estimates published by Sahara (1987a: 282). Second, chariots were adopted from the steppes by 1300 BC, but Chinese armies did not adopt northern or steppe patterns of combat based on an ethos of individual valour. Third, jade weapons in elite burials replaced the bronze weapons which usually accompanied the peoples of the steppes in their graves. Bronze Age China therefore had several aspects which seem to emphasise the ritual side of society, yet warfare and violence were still defining features of the period with numerous finds of bronze weapons in the archaeological record. Moreover, new research has critiqued the traditional emphasis on bronze as centrally distributed prestige goods and emphasised increasing commercialisation in Bronze Age China (Campbell et al. 2021).

With the exception of chariots, the Yayoi cultures of Bronze Age Japan were more receptive to the bronze culture of the steppes than the central plains. Bronze was used for weapons and bells, but not for vessels. Bronze weapons were frequent grave goods in Yayoi elite tombs where they were often found with bronze mirrors. The first bronze mirrors in Japan were imported from Korea and were of northern type. By the latter part of the Yayoi, Chinese bronze mirrors became common and were frequently exchanged within political networks (Edwards 1999). Even during the essentially Iron Age Early Kofun period (AD 250–400), bronze mirrors remained the main symbol of political authority until replaced by iron armour in the fifth century (Sasaki 2017: 68). However, Chinese influence on the use of Yayoi halberds cannot be ruled out (Matsugi 2001: 57; Kobayashi 2017).

A rich record of drawings on Yayoi pots and bronze bells has been much debated. A number of these drawings include figures with shields, halberds and other weapons. There are several examples of two or three warriors who appear to be engaged in combat. A jar from Shimizukaze (Nara) has two human figures each holding shields and halberds (Kobayashi 2017: 138). Other warriors are associated with deer and birds, requiring a broader symbolic interpretation. Such an analysis is beyond the scope of the present Element, but I argue that we must not lose sight of the underlying violence intrinsic to warriors and their depiction in Yayoi society. Figure 11 shows one of the most interesting yet mysterious art works from the Yayoi. There are two overlapping drawings (Kobayashi 2017: 139). On the left is a human figure with a shield and a short halberd. The shield was rubbed out and a deer and two bird-shaped figures were then drawn at right with deeper lines. The larger bird appears to be mounting or even copulating with the deer; a human wearing a bird costume is one possible

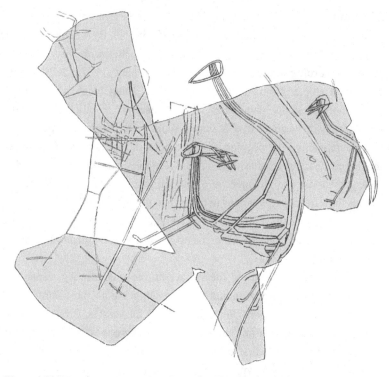

Figure 11 Drawings on pottery from the Karako-kagi site (Nara). Drawn by
J. Uchiyama.

interpretation of this drawing. While the broader meaning remains unclear,
there is a need for further research which integrates questions of ritual and
violence in Yayoi society.

3.2 Weapons and Warfare in Bronze Age Japan

Evidence for warfare in Bronze Age Japan derives from a wide range of
materials including skeletal trauma, weapons, fortifications, burials, artistic
depictions and texts. Although levels of violence in the Neolithic Jōmon period
continue to be debated (Nakao et al. 2016; Hudson et al. 2020), by any criteria
there is abundant evidence for warfare in the Yayoi. A recent compilation based
on existing reports found that more than 3 per cent of skeletons from Yayoi
Japan have evidence of skeletal violence (Nakagawa et al. 2017). This is likely
to be an underestimate since new bioarchaeological protocols for violent trauma
have been developed in recent years (Schulting & Fibiger 2012).

As elsewhere in Eurasia, the Bronze Age saw the introduction of a totally new
set of weapons into Japan. Swords, spears, shields, helmets and armour

provided the main military accoutrements in Japan until the sixteenth century, when guns began to transform warfare (Chase 2003). The major difference in terms of weaponry between Japan and many other parts of Bronze Age Eurasia was the absence of the chariot in the archipelago. Chariots were widely used across Eurasia for a thousand years from around 1700 to 700 BC (Anthony 2007: 18). In the central plains of northern China, chariots were introduced by the thirteenth century BC (Rawson 2017) and were probably present in Mongolia by around the same time (Esin et al. 2021). Chariots are found in Liaoning province in north-east China (Shaughnessy 1988: 190), but never spread beyond to the forested or mountainous regions of Northeast Asia. In Japan, horses were only introduced in the late fourth century AD, when the age of the chariot was long past.

The first Yayoi-period weapons were polished stone daggers and arrowheads of Korean style found at the earliest rice-growing sites in northern Kyushu such as Nabatake (Saga). At Shinmachi (Fukuoka), an Initial Yayoi grave contained a mature male who had been shot from behind with a polished stone arrowhead. Although this dolmen burial shows continental influence in its mortuary style, the skeleton itself is morphologically similar to the Jōmon populations who had long lived in the region. One interpretation of this find might thus be a local hunter-gatherer attacked by incoming farmers. A more complex situation is, however, suggested by the discovery of human teeth from another, younger individual in a pit inside the grave, a find which suggests that the Shinmachi people may have engaged in headhunting (Matsugi 2001: 27–8).

Villages enclosed by ditches and fences were introduced from the Korean peninsula at the beginning of the Yayoi period (Arbousse-Bastide 2005; Mizoguchi 2013). At Itazuke (Fukuoka), a V-shaped ditch 1.5–4.5 m wide and 0.7–2.3 m deep encircled a settlement measuring 81 by 110 m. Some Yayoi sites have earthen banks along the ditches and excavations at Asahi (Aichi) have shown that wooden stakes and barricades were also used (Tanaka 1991: 20–3).

Enclosed villages and stone weapons spread east up the archipelago together with rice farming. In the Osaka–Kyoto region, polished stone weapons were replaced by a chipped stone technology but the shape of the daggers and arrowheads still followed Korean prototypes (Matsugi 2001: 30). In other words, chipped stone weapons imitated polished stone weapons which themselves imitated bronze, a further example of the 'creative translations' of bronzisation.

Around 400 BC, bronze swords, halberds and spearheads began to be introduced to Kyushu. Of the three weapons, swords were the most popular, followed next by halberds; bronze spearheads seem to have been less widely used. In terms of absolute numbers, stone weapons remained more common than bronze but are found mainly from settlement remains and were rarely buried in warrior graves. Evidence for the actual use of bronze swords includes a sword tip found embedded in the skull of a mature female from Neshiko (Nagasaki) (Matsugi 2001: 46). After a period of only three or four centuries, iron weapons also appeared in Japan. Again, the sword appears to have been the weapon of choice. As iron became more common, bronze weapons – as well as bronze bells – were transformed into increasingly oversized and 'ritualised' objects. By the third century AD, iron had replaced bronze and stone weapons.

Even as iron gained ground in Yayoi Japan, however, bronze arrowheads became common from the first century AD, a change which, according to Matsugi (2001: 73), may reflect the influence of Han China, presumably through its commandery at Lelang in Korea. A mould for casting bronze arrowheads has been found at Sugu-okamoto (Fukuoka). Most Yayoi bronze arrowheads are small: less than 4 cm long and around 3 g in weight. Some Japanese scholars once thought that they were too small to have been used in actual warfare, but several skeletons with such arrowheads deeply embedded in the bone have been found at Aoya-kamijichi (Tottori) (Matsugi 2001: 74). Bronze arrowheads of similar size are known in Europe. The 134 bronze arrowheads found at the Late Bronze Age Wrocław–Widawa site in Poland had lengths ranging between 2.8 and 4.8 cm (Baron et al. 2020). In China, small bronze arrowheads were also used with crossbows, which were in use by at least the fourth century BC (Wright 2005). In Japan, a Yayoi-period crossbow part has been found at Himebaranishi (Shimane), although the excavation report concludes that, since it appears less practical than examples from Han China, it was probably a crossbow-shaped ritual artefact (Adachi 1999: 126). Even if this interpretation were correct, however, it would imply that the Yayoi people were familiar with actual crossbows. More than ten three-winged bronze crossbow bolts are known from Yayoi sites located in Okinawa, Nagasaki, Fukuoka, Kagawa and Shimane prefectures (Ashiya Board of Education 2007) (Figure 4).

3.2.1 Organising Warfare

From the late seventh century AD, the Japanese court started to establish a military system based on Tang China (Farris 1995). Prior to that, we know very little about how warfare in the Japanese archipelago was organised and conducted. Matsugi (2001: 47–8) suggests that separate units based on weapons (archers, etc) did not exist in the Yayoi; instead, warriors combined different weapons as available or appropriate. The problem with this interpretation is that many Bronze Age weapons, including swords and shields, would have required special training to be used effectively (Molloy & Horn 2020). Wooden daggers which follow bronze prototypes – some very closely – have been found at Yayoi sites such as Minamikata (Okayama). Mizoguchi (2013: 133–4) regards these as ritual objects but conflates clear weapon-shaped objects with mysterious wooden artefacts of unknown function. Even if these artefacts were found discarded together, we cannot assume that they were necessarily used in the same context. In my view, it is likely that the weapon-shaped wooden objects were used for military training.

Shields, one of the most important inventions of the Bronze Age, were rectangular and made of wood, sometimes covered in lacquer. Yayoi art suggests that shields were at least sometimes held in the hand and used with swords or, more commonly, with halberds.[8] As well as shields, several examples of organic body armour have been found at Yayoi sites including Minamikata, Sasai (Fukuoka) and Iba (Shizuoka) (Ryan & Barnes 2014). Wooden cuirasses painted with red and black lacquer had geometric patterns perhaps designed to frighten opponents (Tanaka 1991: 50). In Europe, it is often assumed that bronze cuirasses developed from organic prototypes, although none of the latter have survived (Mödlinger 2017: 172–3). In Japan, by contrast, no bronze cuirasses are known, perhaps because the metal was so scarce. In the Kofun period, iron armour became common and 530 iron cuirasses are reported from Japan (Ryan & Barnes 2014: 4).

In the early centuries of the Yayoi period, we know from sourcing studies of the lithic materials used to make stone weapons that most conflicts occurred within regional zones such as Kyushu (Matsugi 2001: 38–41). Since bronze was imported and sometimes recast, the scale of conflict becomes harder to evaluate over time. By the third century AD, Chinese accounts of the land of Wa (Japan) mention that 'For some seventy or eighty years . . . there were disturbances and warfare' (Tsunoda & Goodrich 1951). After this unrest, the Wa people are said to have been unified under a queen Pimiko (or Himiko in modern Japanese). Increasing political unification in third-century Japan is often linked to the ritual role of bronze in symbolising power. Sahara (1987b: 50) proposed that Yayoi bronze weapons originally followed continental shapes and had sharp edges, but over time 'weapons to kill with' became ceremonial 'weapons to look at'. This argument is based on the appearance of weapons with wider, unsharpened blades and spearheads which cannot be hafted because casting debris is still found in the socket. A wide blade does not, in itself, mean that a weapon is

---

[8] I thank a reviewer for pointing out that this shows the original function of halberds was apparently lost in the Yayoi. The combination of shields and swords in combat was rare in Japan in later centuries (Friday 2004: 90).

impractical – in fact, a wider blade makes it easier to inflict deeper cuts on an opponent (Gener 2018: 141–2) – but the Yayoi examples discussed by Sahara and others develop into highly impractical objects. Although perhaps less pronounced than in Japan, southern Korea also saw an increased 'ritualisation' of bronze weapons. However, Iwanaga (2018) proposes a fundamental difference between the two regions. In Korea, he argues, bronze was not used for the type of communal rituals which worked towards the consensual social integration of large areas of western Japan. In Iwanaga's reading, as compared to Japan, peninsular politics were marked by greater conflict between early kingdoms and he explains this by the fact that iron spread more rapidly in Korea, leading to more decentralised politics (Iwanaga 2018: 108). Iwanaga's ideas about the role of metals in generating political (de)centralisation are interesting; nevertheless, he perhaps relies too much on the unwarranted assumption that – compared to the more 'political' Koreans – early Japan formed a 'natural' community.

Japanese archaeologists emphasise rice agriculture and associated conflicts over land and water as the fundamental cause of Bronze Age violence; trade with Eurasia and its warrior cultures is rarely considered as a contributing factor. Yet Yayoi warfare clearly developed in the context of close links with the Korean peninsula and cannot only be seen as a natural result of the internal contradictions of agricultural societies in isolation from any broader historical context. This is an area where further research is warranted. Sites such as Haru-no-tsuji site on Iki island may provide some support for this hypothesis. The *Wei zhi* notes that both Tsushima and Iki relied on trade to support poor agricultural production. The fact that the large Yayoi town at Haru-no-tsuji has defensive ditches implies that violence was connected to maritime trade as well as agricultural production.

3.3 Warriors As Heroes?

In European archaeology, Bronze Age warriors have been seen as semi-professional groups who engaged in extensive preparation and training, yet also as symbolically heroic figures governed by particular etiquettes of appearance and behaviour (Treherne 1995; Kristiansen 1999; Kristiansen & Larsson 2005; Schulting 2013). Similarities between Bronze Age warriors and the Homeric epics have been noted (Vandkilde 2006).

In East Asia, a rather different type of Bronze Age warrior ethos has been discussed for China. Keightley (1993) argued that individual hand-to-hand combat using swords was not important to Bronze Age Chinese elites and noted that the early Chinese classics contain no heroic warrior tales like the

Iliad. The Shang seem to have adopted the weapons but not the tactics of the steppes (Rawson 2015, 2017). What, then, about Japan? Did Bronze Age Japan follow the Chinese style of elite warrior culture or another pattern?

In the Middle Ages, there are many heroic warrior narratives from Japan, the most famous being the *Tale of the Heike*. In 1948, historian Shō Ishimoda published an influential essay in which he argued that Hegel's 'Heroic Age' had also existed in ancient Japan. Ishimoda's 'Heroic Age' was a critique of the emperor system and attempted to show that power in ancient Japan did not automatically derive from the imperial line but rather from conflicts between local elites. This critique retains its resonance against the background of reactionary scholars who combine support for the emperor system with an insistence that Japan has been uniquely peaceful in world history, an idea that can be traced back to the writings of Motoori Norinaga (1730–1801) (see Hudson 2021b). For reasons discussed in an important historiographic essay by Isomae (2002), the debate over Japan's ancient 'Heroic Age' went out of fashion after the 1950s, though it was briefly revived by Matsugi (2001).

When we look at the earliest Japanese records, military exploits are frequently narrated in terms of underhand subterfuge – sometimes with a homoerotic subtext – rather than as a professional or heroic struggle. For instance, the *Kojiki* recounts how eighty *Tsuchigumo* or 'Earth Spiders' – a people who resisted the Yamato kingdom and who perhaps lived in pit houses – were murdered at a banquet given by the mythical ruler Jimmu (Philippi 1969: 174–7). The legendary prince Yamato-takeru, the most famous warrior in the early texts, who has been described as an 'Arthurian hero' by Littleton (1995), dressed as a girl in order to kill two Kumaso brothers during a feast, the younger brother being stabbed in the buttocks while making his escape (Philippi 1969: 234–5).[9] Later, Yamato-takeru pledged friendship with a local warrior in Izumo on the Sea of Japan, only to kill him after switching swords after bathing together. When attacking the Kumaso in southern Kyushu, an advisor to Emperor Keikō devised a plan whereby two beautiful daughters of a Kumaso chief were enticed to Keikō's camp by 'valuable presents'. Once in the camp, 'The Emperor straightway had intercourse with [one of the daughters], and made a show of affection for her.' The girl then returned home with strong saké. While her father slept after drinking this saké, the daughter cut his bowstring, allowing him to be killed by the soldiers who had accompanied her. In a note no doubt added to appease Confucian sensibilities, the *Nihon shoki* claims that

---

[9] Located in southern Kyushu, the Kumaso were another 'tribal' group who opposed the Yamato state (see Hudson 1999: 194–7).

Keikō was 'provoked by such excessively unfilial conduct and put [the daughter] to death' (Aston 1972: I, 195–6).

These stories cannot be read literally. However, the implication that the Yamato kingdom found it difficult to subjugate populations away from the alluvial plains unless it resorted to 'underhand' methods has a ring of truth. In the early Japanese texts, the violent exploits of the Yamato heroes are unconvincingly combined with attempts to stress the moral superiority of the court in Chinese (Confucian) terms. Yet early Chinese texts also emphasise the 'underhand' use of swords in ambushes and assassinations (Rawson 2017), raising the question of intertextual influences in early Japanese descriptions of violence.

In a much-cited paper, Treherne (1995) argued that Bronze Age warriors in Europe followed a masculine ethos which involved relationships of honour, patronage and reciprocity, the shared consumption of alcohol and ideals of bodily decoration and grooming. While it would be wrong to force Yayoi Japan into the same mould, there are nevertheless some interesting parallels which may help us to think about the Yayoi in a new way. For Treherne, bronze mirrors were part of a culture of warrior beauty and were associated with other toilet articles such as combs, razors, tweezers and tattooing awls. The *Wei zhi* account of the 'abstainer' mentioned earlier shows that the combing of hair and care of bodily appearance was a social norm, at least in the third century. Bronze mirrors are one of the key artefacts in Yayoi archaeology. Usually seen as ritual objects linked to elite culture and to the later 'imperial regalia', there has been little discussion of the possible cosmetic as opposed to the political use of bronze mirrors.[10] Tattoos are mentioned in the *Wei zhi* and are also depicted on Yayoi pottery. A Late Yayoi jar from Kametsuka (Aichi) has a tattooed human face incised on one side. Similar designs are known from Yayoi sites in Yamaguchi and Kagawa prefectures. The intricate tattoo patterns depicted on these pots were no doubt designed to be seen. Yayoi facial tattoos would have required some type of toilet articles to shave the face and perhaps parts of the head.[11] Aside from mirrors, however, there are few examples of bronze personal ornaments in Yayoi Japan, unlike in the northern steppe zone, where such items are more common.

---

[10] The use of the 'imperial regalia' of mirror, sword and jewel in the enthronement ceremony for the Japanese emperor (cf. Breen 2020) has tended to overdetermine the symbolic importance of these artefacts in Japanese archaeology.

[11] Recent genetic research suggests the scalp hair of Yayoi people was likely thicker than that of populations in the preceding Jōmon period. As well as hair thickness, the *EDARV370A* variant of the human Ectodysplasin receptor is associated with increased eccrine sweat glands and smaller mammary gland fat pad size (Kamberov et al. 2013). Though found in almost all Holocene populations from mainland East Asia and the Americas, this allele is missing from the Jōmon samples analysed by Wang and colleagues (2021).

There has so far been little discussion of the possibility of professional warriors or mercenaries in the Yayoi. Later historical texts contain some relevant comments in this respect. For example, the *Nihon shoki* describes how in the reign of King Ōjin, 'The fishermen [*ama*, literally 'sea people'] of several places clamoured noisily, and would not obey the Imperial command.' While Ōjin is a legendary ruler, it seems likely this description reflects frequent resistance by these 'sea people'. The same text shows that 'fishermen' could became mercenaries, as when the *ama* from Awaji island served a local warlord against the court (Aston 1972: I, 305–6).

Kyushu-type bronze swords and spearheads are found in Korea, raising the possibility that warriors from Japan crossed over to the peninsula (Iwanaga 2018: 110–14), perhaps as mercenaries. This mercenary interpretation is complicated by the fact that some of the Japanese weapons that reached Korea were of non-utilitarian form. Yet, as one reviewer of this Element pointed out, the weapons were part of a broader trade across the Tsushima Straits, and I suggest that warriors of some sort would have been needed to protect that trade. This question relates to one of the most controversial issues in the ancient history of Northeast Asia. Early Japanese chronicles mention the 'Mimana Nihonfu' or 'Japanese government office in Mimana'. Many pre-war historians saw Mimana (or Imna in modern Korean) as a colonial outpost of the Japanese state. Given the violent history of later Japanese invasions and annexation of the peninsula (1592–8 and 1910–45), Korean scholars such as Park (2018: 134) are reluctant to call Imna a colony, but accept its status as an 'administrative office' for envoys from the archipelago. While a detailed analysis of this thorny problem is beyond the scope of this Element, it seems clear that warriors from the Japanese islands were active on the Korean peninsula in some capacity by at least the fourth century AD. These warriors cannot necessarily be called 'Japanese', a term which might imply they were part of an official army of the Yamato state. An inscription on a memorial stele to the Koguryŏ king Kwanggaet'o, erected in 414 in what is now Jilin province in north-east China, uses the term pronounced *Wa* in Japanese (Korean *wae*, Chinese *wo*) (Szczesniak 1951; Hudson 1989). Although Park (2018: 142) insists that the Wa are to be linked with Japan's central polity located in Nara, the reality was probably much more fluid. Based on an analysis of the twelfth-century *Silla pon'gi*, Hatada (1979) argued that the Wa were pirates based in northern Kyushu. This may also be a too limited view. Piracy and trade probably alternated with episodes of more sustained warfare, perhaps focussed on controlling trading entrepôts, resulting in a Wa diaspora on the peninsula which likely comprised a diverse mix of warriors, traders, craftspeople and official envoys from various kingdoms in the archipelago. Interestingly, the opposite possibility of 'Korean' warriors employed in the archipelago is rarely if ever considered. Writing about the fifth to sixth centuries AD, Kameda (2018) argues that groups from the Korean peninsula were employed by chiefs in Okayama on the Seto Inland Sea to produce iron, fabricate tools and supervise maritime transport. If this was the case, then warriors would have been needed to protect that trade and this pattern plausibly dates back to the Bronze Age. Against a background of political competition between regional kingdoms in Yayoi and Kofun Japan, hiring warrior specialists from the peninsula would no doubt have been an attractive option.

4 Bronze Age Island East Asia and the Rise of the Barbarian Niche

Childe (1950) proposed that the Bronze Age marked a decisive shift to an urban and commercial civilisation. Notwithstanding critiques such as Jennings (2016), many historians and archaeologists have followed Childe's approach, with the result that 'areas that do not display these Bronze Age urbanised "civilisational" attributes tend to get marginalised' (Rowlands & Fuller 2018: 173). A common response has been to engage in what Spriggs (2018) calls 'urban-state envy' – boosting or exaggerating the evidence for early civilisations. In Japan, there have even been claims of a 'Jōmon civilisation' (cf. Habu & Fawcett 2008; Hudson 2021b). Using a different perspective, Rowlands and Fuller (2018) regard the focus on the Bronze Age as misplaced, and propose a re-evaluation of the Neolithic for Africa and other parts of the Global South.

If Bronze Age societies typically formed civilisations, however, they also had what Scott (2017: 248–52) calls their 'dark twins' in the shape of barbarian societies, a relationship articulated by Lattimore (1962) and by classical writers such as Strabo (Horden & Purcell 2000: 157). The underlying political economy is nicely summarised by Liu and colleagues (2018: 105): 'Most major Bronze Age civilizations developed in the catchments of large rivers that were sustaining a high population density through intensive agriculture. These areas, however, are almost always devoid of mineral resources, which are typically exposed only in mountainous areas, remote from the centres of agricultural civilization. Thus, these centres were dependent on distant areas to provide their strategically important metals, primarily copper, tin and gold, but also lead and silver.' As well as metals, Bronze Age East Asia developed extensive trade in salt, textiles (silk), slaves, jade, amber, shells, bronze weapons and mirrors, and perhaps timber. While various elements of the macro-regional division of labour in East Asia remain unclear, I have termed these dynamic changes the 'secondary people's revolution' (Hudson 2020a).

The present Element has focussed especially on areas of eastern Eurasia which were slow to develop the Childean traits of Bronze Age civilisation. From Scott (2017), I borrow the term *barbarian* to refer to peoples on the margins of the alluvial civilisations of East Asia. Most of this Element has focussed on Island East Asia – the islands off the east coast of Eurasia from Taiwan to the Kurils. From the perspective of the mainland 'core' states, these islands were remote, mountainous lands which lay beyond the reasonable possibility of conquest given the technologies of the time. Even in the thirteenth century, Mongol armies failed in their attacks on Kyushu and had considerable difficulty in subduing the Ainu on Sakhalin. Within Island East Asia, a series of mini-states developed in the alluvial plains of western Japan and then – in the Middle Ages – the Kantō region around modern Tokyo. These mini-states were surrounded by ungovernable 'barbarian' societies of the seas and mountains. In order to emphasise its own coreness, the ancient Japanese state adopted or invented Chinese-style names and categories such as *tennō* ('emperor') and its own barbarians of the four cardinal directions (Hudson 1999; Batten 2003; Amino 2012). To the extent that these Japanese conceits followed proper Confucian precepts – and the Japanese kings payed tribute – they were generally accepted by the Chinese, who were far more concerned with non-state actors. For chiefs and kings in the archipelago, participation in the Chinese tributary system provided material gifts such as bronze mirrors, but 'what the Japanese leaders were really after was the official Chinese recognition such gifts implied, which reinforced their legitimacy at home and helped them consolidate their rule' (Batten 2012: 92).

Building on previous studies such as Yü (1967) and Di Cosmo (2002), Barnes (2007) has analysed how Han and Wei China impacted the Japanese islands between the second century BC and the third century AD. In 108 BC, the Han invaded northern Korea and established a commandery at Lelang near modern P'yŏngyang (Byington 2014). Designed initially to limit the power of steppe barbarians to threaten China, this invasion brought some Japanese kingdoms into the Han tributary network by AD 57 (Barnes 2007: 5). However, the real growth of state power in Japan occurred after the fall of the Wei in 265 led to a power vacuum in Korea and to competition between the kingdoms of the peninsula and the archipelago. The Kofun period began exactly at this time when Japan was no longer mentioned in Chinese dynastic records for almost two centuries between 266 and 421.

The insularity of Island East Asia worked both for *and* against the barbarian condition. Japan was one of the barbarian 'stars' in premodern East Asia, the principal home to the *wakō*, a shifting category of raiders and traders. *Wakō* included Koreans and Chinese, yet 'Japanese tended to serve as a common language among *wakō*, and most of their bases were in Japan because of the absence of strong central authority there until the end of the sixteenth century' (Smits 2019: 40). The Kwanggaet'o stele suggests *wakō* raiding (broadly interpreted) may stretch back to at least the fourth century AD. Taiwan saw short-lived colonial outposts of Dutch and Spanish rule in the seventeenth century, but Aboriginal Austronesians and various Chinese and Japanese pirates maintained a decentralised tribal society there until the Japanese colonisation of 1895–1945. Outside powers only managed to 'open' Japan from the mid-nineteenth century and the American occupation from 1945 to 1952 (or 1972 in the case of Okinawa) was the first time the archipelago was controlled by a foreign power. The northern islands of Hokkaido, Sakhalin and the Kurils were not directly colonised by Japan and Russia until the nineteenth century. Prior to its industrial settler colonialism, Japan attempted to exploit these islands around the Sea of Okhotsk through long-distance trade, yet the Ainu maintained a vigorous trading diaspora until the seventeenth century. The *wakō* and the Ainu were two of the most successful non-state actors in premodern Island East Asia. However, insularity also meant that the possibilities for Island East Asian groups to feed off states were more limited than those available to the nomadic societies of Inner Eurasia.

In comparing civilisation and its barbarian 'twin', I do not mean to suggest that either condition was fixed or rigid; both conditions could encompass considerable variation (see e.g. Hudson 2020a; Campbell et al. 2021). The fluid dialectic between civilisation and barbarian analysed by scholars such as Barnes, Di Cosmo, Smits and Yü is rejected by the neo-Toynbeean proponents of Japanese 'civilisation theory' (cf. Morris-Suzuki 1993; Hudson 2021b). A key figure in that movement, archaeologist Yoshinori Yasuda (2008), portrays the East Asian Bronze Age as a 'clash of civilisations', claiming that an 'invasion of the wheat/foxtail millet cultivating and pastoral people' into northern China led to the collapse of civilisation in the Yangtze region and to migrations by rice farmers to the south and east. Such ideas resemble those of earlier generations of scholars writing about 'Aryan' invasions (cf. Anthony 2007; Demoule 2014), yet Yasuda takes the argument to even greater extremes, insisting that the history of East Asia since 2000 BC has been one of the 'oppression and destruction of the rice-cultivating piscatory people's "civiliza-tion of beauty and compassion" by the wheat/barley/millet-cultivating pastoral people's "civilization of force and conflict"' (Yasuda 2013: 462). The research summarised in this Element points to a very different set of conclusions. West Eurasian domesticated crops and animals certainly had a major impact on East Asia in the Bronze Age, but evidence from ancient DNA suggests there was no large-scale migration by western pastoralists into the eastern steppes or beyond

(Damgaard et al. 2018; Jeong et al. 2020). Local populations in East Asia themselves actively adopted the new foods and technologies. Population movements certainly occurred within the East Asian region, but these were primarily migrations by peoples who had lived there since at least the Neolithic (Ning et al. 2020). There were no opposing rice or wheat/millet 'civilisations' as proposed by Yasuda. While these crops did originate in different places, they began to spread in the Neolithic and by the Bronze Age had become integrated into increasingly 'globalised' multicropping systems. This is nowhere clearer than in the Japanese islands where cereal agriculture only developed through the adoption of a diverse suite of Eurasian crops and animals. Another clear conclusion is that rice farmers in East Asia were not fishers. While carp aquaculture began as early as eight thousand years ago and by the Bronze Age was probably widely associated with rice paddy fields, carp likely provided a relatively minor addition to the diet.[12] The evidence from Japan shows that more intensive fishing was carried out by specialist maritime groups who traded fish, shellfish and salt with farmers. Finally, the analysis of violence in the Japanese islands in Section 3 of this Element clearly demonstrates that rice farmers cannot be categorised as exemplars of a peaceful 'civilisation of beauty and compassion'!

More broadly, the Bronze Age was a time of new, transcultural identities rather than fixed civilisations in the Victorian mode. As argued by Vandkilde (2016), bronzisation can be understood as a type of premodern globalisation. Here, I have stressed certain similarities found across Eurasia but I have also noted that the process of bronzisation engendered differences or what Rawson (2017) calls 'reception and resistance'. Among other things, this perspective suggests a quite different interpretation of Japanese prehistory than commonly presented. Many scholars assume that in the Neolithic the archipelago was home to a single cultural horizon known as the Jōmon. While there is certainly debate over the details, the same Jōmon label is usually applied to the whole archipelago – except for Okinawa, where the terms 'Ryukyu Jōmon' or 'Shell Mound period' are also used. In the Bronze Age, by contrast, it is assumed that several different cultures evolved, breaking up the previous cultural unity of the islands. As discussed earlier in this Element, the presence or absence of wet-rice farming is used to separate the cultures of Hokkaido and Okinawa from the 'mainstream' of the Japanese historical experience. In my view,

---

[12] While the dietary contribution may have been minor, the fish were no doubt a welcome addition to peasant foodways. During my own fieldwork on paddy field carp aquaculture in Nagano in the central highlands of Japan, I was told that as late as the mid-twentieth century, villagers would sometimes cook and eat dried herring which had been purchased as fertilizer.

however, the complete opposite interpretation is more appropriate. In the Jōmon, there was a loosely connected series of 'Neolithicities' (Fuller & Carretero 2018) found across the archipelago. The Bronze Age, by contrast, was the first time when all of Japan from Okinawa up to Rebun island was really connected in the same expanding world. The cultures and societies of Bronze Age 'Japan' were not the same but were participating in one connected world.

4.1 Niche Construction and the Barbarian

Critics of James Scott's *Against the Grain* have argued that he replaces traditional metanarratives of the rise of the state with an equally simplistic or 'flat' counter-narrative of what we might call the *meta-barbarian*. A series of essays in this vein, mostly by Americanist archaeologists, was published in 2019 in the *Cambridge Archaeological Journal*. Scott (2019: 720–1) himself accepts that the people he glosses as 'barbarian' encompass a wide range of shifting economies, relations with neighbouring states and ecologies. In this Element, I have tried to make some preliminary observations about the time and space of the barbarian condition. Using the work of Kristiansen, Vandkilde and others, I have emphasised the role of the Bronze Age in generating the first barbarian economies. As noted already, this raises the question of whether or not barbarians *sensu* Scott can be said to exist in places such as Africa which remained 'outside' the Bronze Age (cf. Rowlands & Fuller 2018). This is a question for further research but, given the role of the state in spawning resistance from non-state actors, a reasonable hypothesis is that the barbarian was ultimately a global phenomenon.

Recent archaeology has paid growing attention to how our species has impacted the world through construction of a 'human niche' (Rowley-Conwy & Layton 2011; Ellis 2015; Boivin et al. 2016). In East Asia, as elsewhere, research has focussed on major environmental turning points such as the Neolithic, urbanisation and industrialisation (Bleed & Matsui 2010; Aikens & Lee 2013; Hudson 2020b; Storozum et al. 2020). Less attention has been given to the Bronze Age, but the expansion in Eurasian trade networks from the third millennium BC onwards was associated with new environmental adaptations including steppe pastoralism and milking cultures. Domesticated cereals and animals became increasingly globalised. Deforestation was associated with metal production, urbanisation and pastoralism (Chew 2001; Kristiansen 2006). These new economic activities represented a significant expansion and intensification of human niche construction. Barbarians – in the sense used here – relied on this Bronze Age economic infrastructure in order to expand their niche. The barbarian niche relied above all on trade; Horden and Purcell (2000: 158) quip that markets were as important as muscle. In his environmental history of China, Elvin (2004: 25) claims that 'Barbarians were good for the environment,' but the extent to which the barbarian niche really slowed environmental degradation as compared to neighbouring civilisations is a question for future research.

Finally, it is important to note that *barbarian* cannot be simply equated with state-centric views of uncultured or brutish people. Barbarian does not mean artistic sensibilities were inferior. Several examples of Bronze Age art in Japan have been examined in this Element. While Neolithic Japan is known for its highly imaginative and abstract art found on Jōmon pots and figurines, in the Yayoi pictorial art became almost entirely figurative. In both its style and contents (warriors, animals, ships), Yayoi art displays striking similarities to Bronze Age art from Europe. These similarities do not necessarily mean that there were direct influences between the two regions; rather, the convergence is perhaps to be understood as part of a shared process of bronzisation. In this respect it is interesting to note experimental work finding that whereas social isolation leads to greater abstraction in art, social contact encourages figurative styles which are transparent to outsiders (Granito et al. 2019).

Section 3 of this Element discussed evidence for violence and warriors in Bronze Age Japan. It is clear that the Japanese islands were a violent place during the Yayoi period, but we need to remember that violence is a historically contingent phenomenon (Dwyer & Damousi 2020). Although it is difficult to analyse past experiences of violence without texts, we must assume that Yayoi and other barbarian societies developed various meanings and critiques of those experiences. Since at least Elias' 1939 work *The Civilising Process*, an influential strand in social theory has argued that from the Enlightenment era the state – aka 'civilisation' – has controlled and ultimately reduced violence (Elias 1994; Pinker 2011). Recent research has nuanced this narrative (Skoda 2013; Carroll 2017; Dwyer 2017; Fibiger 2018). If the barbarian can be understood as a position vis-à-vis the state, then violence was less a default condition and more a part of the 'art of not being governed' (Scott 2009).

As noted in the Introduction, several arguments in this Element have been provisional, provocative and probably controversial. My main objective has been to use comparative archaeology to suggest that the historical evolution of East Asia from the third millennium BC to the beginning of the first millennium AD was part of a Eurasia-wide process of bronzisation. I have adopted James Scott's usage of the term 'barbarian' to attempt to recentre (or re-marginalise) those Bronze Age peoples who lived in positions of resistance to the increasingly powerful alluvial grain states of East Asia. While aspects of my thesis will no doubt be disputed, my hope is that this Element will nevertheless provide an approach to ancient East Asia which goes beyond the nation-state and points towards a more fluid and dynamic Eurasian history.

Bibliography

Unless otherwise noted, all Japanese books are published in Tokyo.

Adachi, K., ed. (1999). *Himebaranishi iseki* [*The Himebaranishi Site*]. Matsue: Ministry of Construction Matsue Office and Shimane Prefecture Board of Education.

Adachi, K. (2011). *Kōjindani iseki: Izumo ni mainō sareta tairyō no seidōki* [*The Kōjindani Site and the Large Quantity of Bronzes Deposited in Izumo*]. Dōseisha.

Ahn, S.-M. (2010). The emergence of rice agriculture in Korea: archaeobotanical perspectives. *Archaeological and Anthropological Sciences*, 2, 89–98.

Aikens, C. M., & Lee, G.-A. (2013). Postglacial inception and growth of anthropogenic landscapes in China, Korea, Japan and the Russian Far East. *Anthropocene*, 4, 46–56.

Amino, Y. (2012). *Rethinking Japanese History*. Ann Arbor: Center for Japanese Studies, University of Michigan.

An, Z. (1991). Continental roots of the earliest Japanese culture. In K. Hanihara, ed., *Japanese As a Member of the Asian and Pacific Populations*. Kyoto: International Research Center for Japanese Studies, pp. 173–86.

Anderson, K. (2018). Becoming the warrior: constructed identity or functional identity? In C. Horn & K. Kristiansen, eds., *Warfare in Bronze Age Society*. Cambridge: Cambridge University Press, pp. 213–28.

Anthony, D. W. (2007). *The Horse, the Wheel, and Language: How Bronze Age Riders from the Eurasian Steppes Shaped the Modern World*. Princeton, NJ: Princeton University Press.

Aomori [Archaeology Centre & Prefecture], eds. (1985). *Tareyanagi iseki hakkutsu chōsa hōkokusho* [*Report on Excavations at the Tareyanagi Site*]. Aomori City: Aomori Prefecture Board of Education.

Arbousse-Bastide, T. (2005). *Les structures d'habitat enclos de la Protohistoire du Japon (période de Yayoi 350 BC–300 AD)*. BAR International Series 1345. Oxford: Archaeopress.

Ardalan, A., Oskarsson, M., Natanaelsson, C., Wilton, A. N., Ahmadian, A. & Savolainen, P. (2012). Narrow genetic basis for the Australian dingo confirmed through analysis of paternal ancestry. *Genetica*, 140, 65–73.

Armit, I. (2020). Ritual violence and headhunting in Iron Age Europe. In G. G. Fagan, L. Fibiger, M. Hudson & M. Trundle, eds., *The Cambridge World History of Violence, Volume 1: The Prehistoric and Ancient Worlds*. Cambridge: Cambridge University Press, pp. 441–59.

Ashiya Board of Education (2007). *Ashiya-shi shitei bunkazai: Ege-no-yama iseki shutsudo seidōsei kanshiki sanyokuzoku* [*Ashiya City Designated Cultural Property: The Han Style Bronze Three-Winged Arrowhead from the Ege-no-yama Site*]. Online document: www.city.ashiya.lg.jp/gakushuu/documents/sanyokuzoku.pdf

Aston, W. G. (1972). *Nihongi: Chronicles of Japan from the Earliest Times to AD 697*. Tokyo: Tuttle.

Atwell, W. S. (2005). Another look at silver imports into China, ca. 1635–1644. *Journal of World History*, 16, 467–89.

Autiero, S., & Cobb, M. A., eds. (2021). *Globalization and Transculturality from Antiquity to the Pre-modern World*. London: Routledge.

Balme, J., O'Connor, S. & Fallon, S. (2018). New dates on dingo bones from Madura cave provide oldest firm evidence for arrival of the species in Australia. *Scientific Reports*, 8, e9933.

Barnes, G. L. (2007). *State Formation in Japan: Emergence of a 4th-Century Ruling Elite*. London: Routledge.

Barnes, G. L. (2014). A hypothesis for early Kofun rulership. *Japan Review*, 27, 3–29.

Barnes, G. L. (2015). *Archaeology of East Asia: The Rise of Civilization in China, Korea and Japan*. Oxford: Oxbow.

Baron, J., Puziewicz, J., Nowak, K., Sych, D., Miazga, B. & Ziobro, M. (2020). Same but different: composition, production and use of bronze arrowheads from the Late Bronze Age deposit from Wrocław-Widawa in SW Poland. *Journal of Archaeological Science: Reports*, 32, 102459.

Barras, C. (2019). History of violence. *New Scientist*, 30 March, 29–33.

Batten, B. L. (2003). *To the Ends of Japan: Premodern Frontiers, Boundaries, and Interactions*. Honolulu: University of Hawai'i Press.

Batten, B. L. (2012). Early Japan and the continent. In K. F. Friday, ed., *Japan Emerging: Premodern History to 1850*. Boulder, CO: Westview, pp. 89–97.

Bauer, M. (2017). Religion in Nara and Heian Japan. In K. F. Friday, ed., *Routledge Handbook of Premodern Japanese History*. London: Routledge, pp. 233–47.

Bausch, I. (2017). Prehistoric networks across the Korea strait (5000–1000 BCE): 'early globalization' during the Jomon period in northwest Kyushu? In T. Hodos, ed., *The Routledge Handbook of Archaeology and Globalization*. London: Routledge, pp. 413–37.

Bellwood, P. (2013). *First Migrants: Ancient Migration in Global Perspective*. Chichester: Wiley-Blackwell.

Bellwood, P. (2017). *First Islanders: Prehistory and Human Migration in Island Southeast Asia*. Chichester: Wiley-Blackwell.

Bleed, P., & Matsui, A. (2010). Why didn't agriculture develop in Japan? A consideration of Jomon ecological style, niche construction, and the origins of domestication. *Journal of Archaeological Method and Theory*, 17, 356–70.

Bocquet-Appel, J.-P. (2011). When the world's population took off: the springboard of the Neolithic Demographic Transition. *Science*, 333, 560–1.

Boivin, N., & Frachetti, M., eds., (2018). *Globalization in Prehistory: Contact, Exchange, and the 'People without History'*. Cambridge: Cambridge University Press.

Boivin, N., Zeder, M. A., Fuller, D. Q., Crowther, A., Larson, G., Erlandson, J. M., Denham, T. & Petraglia, M. D. (2016). Ecological consequences of human niche construction: examining long-term anthropogenic shaping of global species distributions. *Proceedings of the National Academy of Sciences USA*, 113(23), 6388–96.

Bouckaert, R. R., Bowern, C. & Atkinson, Q. D. (2018). The origin and expansion of Pama-Nyungan languages across Australia. *Nature Ecology & Evolution*, 2, 741–9.

Bowdler, S. (1995). Offshore islands and maritime explorations in Australian prehistory. *Antiquity*, 69, 945–58.

Breen, J. (2020). The quality of emperorship in 21st century Japan: reflections on the Reiwa accession. *The Asia-Pacific Journal/Japan Focus*, 18, e5404 (https://apjjf.org/2020/12/Breen.html).

Briard, J. (1965). *Les dépôts Bretons et l'age du bronze atlantique*. Rennes: Faculté des Sciences de Rennes.

Broodbank, C. (2010). 'Ships a-sail from over the rim of the sea': voyaging, sailing and the making of Mediterranean societies c. 3500–500 BC. In A. Anderson, J. H. Barrett and K. Boyle, eds., *The Global Origins and Development of Seafaring*. Cambridge: McDonald Institute for Archaeological Research, pp. 249–64.

Broodbank, C. (2011). The Mediterranean and the Mediterranean world in the age of Andrew Sherratt. In T. C. Wilkinson, S. Sherratt and J. Bennet, eds., *Interweaving Worlds: Systemic Interactions in Eurasia, 7th to 1st Millennia BC*. Oxford: Oxbow, pp. 27–36.

Brunson, K., He, N. & Dai, X. (2016). Sheep, cattle, and specialization: new zooarchaeological perspectives on the Taosi Longshan. *International Journal of Osteoarchaeology*, 26, 460–75.

Bulbeck, D. (2008). An integrated perspective on the Austronesian diaspora: the switch from cereal agriculture to maritime foraging in the colonisation of Island Southeast Asia. *Australian Archaeology*, 67, 31–51.

Byington, M., ed. (2013). *The Han Commanderies in Early Korean History*. Cambridge MA: Early Korea Project, Korea Institute, Harvard University.

Campbell, R. B. (2018). *Violence, Kinship and the Early Chinese State: The Shang and Their World*. Cambridge: Cambridge University Press.

Campbell, R. B. (2020). Beyond meaning: skeuomorphy and the mediation of Shang things. *World Archaeology*, 52, 376–94.

Campbell, R. B., Jaffe, Y., Kim, C., Sturm, C. & Jaang, L. (2021). Chinese Bronze Age political economies: a complex polity provisioning approach. *Journal of Archaeological Research*. doi.org/10.1007/s10814-021-09158-0

Carroll, S. (2017). Thinking with violence. *History & Theory*, 55, 23–43.

Chang, K.-C. (1983). *Art, Myth, and Ritual*. Cambridge, MA: Harvard University Press.

Chang, K-C. (1989). Ancient China and its anthropological significance. In C. C. Lamberg-Karlovsky, ed., *Archaeological Thought in America*. Cambridge: Cambridge University Press, pp. 155–66.

Chase, K. (2003). *Firearms: A Global History to 1700*. Cambridge: Cambridge University Press.

Chen, K., Mei, J., Rehren, T. & Zhao, C. (2016). Indigenous production and interregional exchange: late second-millennium BC bronzes from the Hanzhong basin, China. *Antiquity*, 90, 665–78.

Chernykh, E. N. (1992). *Ancient Metallurgy in the USSR: The Early Metal Age*. Cambridge: Cambridge University Press.

Chew, S. C. (2001). *World Ecological Degradation: Accumulation, Urbanization, and Deforestation, 3000 BC–AD 2000*. Walnut Creek, CA: AltaMira Press.

Childe, V. G. (1930). *The Bronze Age*. Cambridge: Cambridge University Press.

Childe, V. G. (1950). The urban revolution. *Town Planning Review*, 21, 3–17.

Choy, K., & Richards, M. P. (2009). Stable isotope evidence of human diet at the Nukdo shell midden site, South Korea. *Journal of Archaeological Science*, 36, 1312–18.

Cramp, L. J. E., Jones, J., Sheridan, A., Smyth, J., Whelton, H., Mulville, J., Sharples, N. & Evershed, R. P. (2014). Immediate replacement of fishing with dairying by the earliest farmers of the northeast Atlantic archipelagos. *Proceedings of the Royal Society B*, 281, e20132372.

Crawford, G. W., Underhill, A., Zhao, Z., Lee, G.-A., Feinman, G., Nicholas, L., Luan, F., Yu, H., Fang, H. & Cai, F. (2005). Late Neolithic plant remains from northern China: preliminary results from Liangchengzhen, Shandong. *Current Anthropology*, 46, 309–17.

Crema, E. R., Habu, J., Kobayashi, K. & Madella, M. (2016). Summed probability distribution 14 C dates suggests regional divergence in the population dynamics of the Jomon period in eastern Japan. *PLoS ONE*, 11(4), e0154809.

Crema, E. R. & Kobayashi, K. (2020). A multi-proxy inference of Jōmon population dynamics using Bayesian phase models, residential data, and summed probability distribution of 14 C dates. *Journal of Archaeological Science*, 117, 105136.

Cunliffe, B. (2008). *Europe between the Oceans: Themes and Variations, 9000 BC–AD 1000*. New Haven, CT: Yale University Press.

d'Alpoim Guedes, J., Jin, G. & Bocinsky, R. K. (2015). The impact of climate on the spread of rice to north-eastern China: a new look at the data from Shandong province. *PLoS ONE*, 10, e0130430.

Damgaard, P. B. Martiniano, R., Kamm, J. et al. (2018). The first horse herders and the impact of early Bronze Age steppe expansions into Asia. *Science*, 360, eaar7711.

Deal, W. E. (2017). Religion in archaic Japan. In K. F. Friday, ed., *Routledge Handbook of Premodern Japanese History*. London: Routledge, pp. 187–201.

de Boer, E., Yang, M. A., Kawagoe, A. & Barnes, G. L. (2020). Japan considered from the hypothesis of farmer/language spread. *Evolutionary Human Sciences*, 2, e13.

Demoule, J.-P. (2014). *Mais où sont passes les Indo-Européens? Le mythe d'origine de l'Occident*. Paris: Seuil.

Di Cosmo, N. (2002). *Ancient China and Its Enemies*. Cambridge: Cambridge University Press.

Di Cosmo, N., & Maas, M. (2018). Introduction. In N. Di Cosmo and M. Maas, eds., *Empires and Exchanges in Eurasian Late Antiquity: Rome, China, Iran, and the Steppe, ca. 250–750*. Cambridge: Cambridge University Press, pp. 1–15.

Diamond, J. (1988). Express train to Polynesia. *Nature*, 336, 307–8.

Drennan, R. D., Peterson, C. E. & Berrey, C. A. (2020). Environmental risk buffering in Chinese Neolithic villages: impacts on community structure in the central plains and the western Liao valley. *Archaeological Research in Asia*, 21, e100165.

Dwyer, P. (2017). Violence and its histories: meanings, methods, problems. *History & Theory*, 55, 7–22.

Dwyer, P., & Damousi, J. (2020). General introduction: violence in world history. In G. G. Fagan, L. Fibiger, M. J. Hudson and M. Trundle, eds., *The Cambridge World History of Violence, Volume 1: The Prehistoric and Ancient Worlds*. Cambridge: Cambridge University Press, pp. 1–18.

Dyakonov, V. M., Pestereva, K. A., Stepanov, A. D. & Mason, O. K. (2019). The spread of metal and metal production technology in the Far Northeast and Alaska over the second millennium BC to the first millennium AD. *World Archaeology*, 51, 355–81.

Edwards, W. (1999). Mirrors on ancient Yamato. *Monumenta Nipponica*, 54, 75–110.

Egami, N. (1964). The formation of the people and the origin of the state in Japan. *Memoirs of the Research Department of the Toyo Bunko*, 23, 35–70.

Elias, N. (1994). *The Civilizing Process*. Oxford: Blackwell.

Ellis, E. C. (2015). Ecology in an anthropogenic biosphere. *Ecological Monographs*, 85, 287–331.

Elvin, M. (2004). *The Retreat of the Elephants: An Environmental History of China*. New Haven: Yale University Press.

Esin, Y., Magail, J., Gantulga, J.-O. & Yeruul-Erdene, C. (2021). Chariots in the Bronze Age of central Mongolia based on the materials from the Khoid Tamir river valley. *Archaeological Research in Asia*, 27, e100304.

Evans, N. & Jones, R. (1997). The cradle of the Pama-Nyungans: archaeological and linguistic speculations. In P. McConvell and N. Evans, eds., *Archaeology and Linguistics: Aboriginal Australia in Global Perspective*. Oxford: Oxford University Press, pp. 385–417.

Fagan, G. G., Fibiger, L., Hudson, M. J. & Trundle, M. eds. (2020). *The Cambridge World History of Violence, Volume 1: The Prehistoric and Ancient Worlds*. Cambridge: Cambridge University Press.

Farris, W. W. (1995). *Heavenly Warriors: The Evolution of Japan's Military, 500–1300*. Revised ed. Cambridge, MA: Council on East Asian Studies, Harvard University.

Fibiger, L. (2018). The past as a foreign country, bioarchaeological perspectives on Pinker's 'prehistoric anarchy'. *Historical Reflections*, 44, 6–16.

Fitzhugh, B., Gjesfjeld, E., Brown, W., Hudson, M. & Shaw, J. (2016). Resilience and the population history of the Kuril Islands, northwest Pacific: a study in complex human ecodynamics. *Quaternary International*, 419, 165–93.

Fitzhugh, B. & Kennett, D. J. (2010). Seafaring intensity and island-mainland interaction along the Pacific coast of North America. In A. Anderson, J. H. Barrett & K. V. Boyle, eds., *The Global Origins and Development of Seafaring*. Cambridge: McDonald Institute for Archaeological Research, pp. 69–80.

Flad, R., Zhu, J., Wang, C., Chen, P., von Falkenhausen, L., Sun, Z. & Li, S. (2005). Archaeological and chemical evidence for early salt production in China. *Proceedings of the National Academy of Sciences USA*, 102, 12618–22.

Fogel, J. A. (2013). *Japanese Historiography and the Gold Seal of 57 C.E. Relic, Text, Object, Fake*. Leiden: Brill.

Frank, A. G. (1993). Bronze Age world system cycles. *Current Anthropology*, 34, 383–429.

Friday, K. F. (2004). *Samurai, Warfare and the State in Early Medieval Japan*. London: Routledge.

Fujimoto, T. (1988). *Mō futatsu no Nihon bunka: Hokkaidō to nantō no bunka* [*Two Other Japanese Cultures: The Cultures of Hokkaido and the Southern Islands*]. Tokyo University Press.

Fujio, S. (2000). Appendix I: the relationship between Kaya and Silla and western Japan in terms of iron production from the first century BC to the sixth century AD. *Journal of East Asian Archaeology*, 2, 96–103.

Fujio, S. (2013). The frame of the Yayoi culture: is wet rice cultivation with irrigation system an indicator of the Yayoi culture? *Bulletin of the National Museum of Japanese History*, 178, 85–120 (in Japanese with English summary).

Fujio, S. (2015). *Yayoi jidai no rekishi* [*The History of the Yayoi Period*]. Kōdansha.

Fujio, S. (2021). Early grain cultivation and starting processes in the Japanese archipelago. *Quaternary*, 4, quat4010003.

Fuller, D. Q., & Carretero, L.G. (2018). The archaeology of Neolithic cooking traditions: archaeobotanical approaches to baking, boiling and fermenting. *Archaeology International*, 21, 109–21.

Gansu Provincial Cultural Relics Work Team, Ningxia Hui Autonomous Region & Dongxiang Autonomous County (1984). Gansu Dongxiang Linjia yizhi fajue baogao (Report of excavations at the Linjia site in Dongxiang, Gansu Province). In *Kaoguxue Jikan* (Archaeological Bulletin). Beijing: China Social Science Press.

Gener, M. (2018). Carp's-tongue swords and their use: functional, technological and morphological aspects. In C. Horn and K. Kristiansen, eds., *Warfare in Bronze Age Society*. Cambridge: Cambridge University Press, pp. 136–52.

Granito, C., Tehrani, J., Kendall, J. & Scott-Phillips, T. (2019). Style of pictorial representation is shaped by intergroup contact. *Evolutionary Human Sciences*, 1, e8.

Greenfield, H. J. (2010). The secondary products revolution: the past, the present and the future. *World Archaeology*, 42(1), 29–54.

Haak, W. Lazaridis, I., Patterson, N. et al. (2015). Massive migration from the steppe was a source for Indo-European languages in Europe. *Nature*, 522, 207–11.

Habu, J. (2010). Seafaring and the development of cultural complexity in northeast Asia: evidence from the Japanese archipelago. In A. Anderson, J. H. Barrett & K. V. Boyle, eds., *The Global Origins and Development of Seafaring*. Cambridge: McDonald Institute for Archaeological Research, pp. 159–89.

Habu, J., & Fawcett, C. (2008). Science or narratives? Multiple interpretations of the Sannai Maruyama site, Japan. In J. Habu, C. Fawcett & J. M. Matsunaga, eds., *Evaluating Multiple Narratives: Beyond Nationalist, Colonialist, Imperialist Archaeologies*. New York: Springer, pp. 91–117.

Harding, A. (2021). *Salt: White Gold in Early Europe*. Cambridge: Cambridge University Press.

Harunari, H. (1991). From figure into sign. *Bulletin of the National Museum of Japanese History*, 35, 3–65 (in Japanese with English summary).

Hashiguchi, T. (2007). *Yayoi jidai no tatakai: tatakai no jittai to kenryoku kikō no seisei* [*Conflict in the Yayoi Period: The Reality of Battle and the Reproduction of the Mechanisms of Power*]. Yūzankaku.

Hatada, T. (1979). An interpretation of the king Kwanggaet'o inscription. *Korean Studies*, 3, 1–17.

Hayama, S. (2020). Balance scales of the Yayoi period seen from archaeological artifacts: taking clues from Nakao Tomoyuki's article. *Kōkogaku Kenkyū*, 67, 82–93 (in Japanese with English summary).

Higham, C. F. W. (2019). A maritime route brought first farmers to mainland Southeast Asia. In C. Wu & B.V. Rolett, eds., *Prehistoric Maritime Cultures and Seafaring in East Asia*. New York: Springer, pp. 41–52.

Higham, C. F. W. & Cawte, H. (2021). Bronze metallurgy in Southeast Asia with particular reference to northeast Thailand. *Journal of World Prehistory*, 34, 1–46.

Higham, C., Higham, T. & Kijngam, A. (2011). Cutting a Gordian knot: the Bronze Age of Southeast Asia: origins, timing and impact. *Antiquity*, 85, 583–98.

Hirosaki [City Board of Education], eds., (1999). *Sunazawa iseki hakkutsu chōsa hōkokusho* [*Report on Excavations at the Sunazawa Site*]. Hirosaki: Hirosaki City Board of Education.

Hiscock, P. (2008). *Archaeology of Ancient Australia*. London: Routledge.

Hiscock, P., & Maloney, T. (2017). Australian lithic technology: evolution, dispersion and connectivity. In T. Hodos, ed., *The Routledge Handbook of Archaeology and Globalization*. London: Routledge, pp. 301–18.

Horden, P., & Purcell, N. (2000). *The Corrupting Sea: A Study of Mediterranean History*. Oxford: Blackwell.

Horiuchi, A., Miyata, Y., Kamijo, N., Cramp, L. & Evershed, R. (2015). A dietary study of the Kamegaoka culture population during the Final Jomon period, Japan, using stable isotope and lipid analyses of ceramic residues. *Radiocarbon*, 57, 721–36.

Horn, C., & Kristiansen, K. (2018). Introducing Bronze Age warfare. In C. Horn and K. Kristiansen, eds., *Warfare in Bronze Age Society*. Cambridge: Cambridge University Press, pp. 1–15.

Hosner, D., Wagner, M., Tarasov, P. E., Chen, X. & Leipe, C. (2016). Spatiotemporal distribution patterns of archaeological sites in China during the Neolithic and Bronze Age: an overview. *Holocene*, 26, 1576–93.

Hudson, M. J. (1989). Ethnicity in East Asian archaeology: approaches to the Wa. *Archaeological Review from Cambridge*, 8, 51–63.

Hudson, M. J. (1990). From Toro to Yoshinogari: changing perspectives on Yayoi period archeology. In G. L. Barnes, ed., *Hoabinhian, Jomon, Yayoi, Early Korean States: Bibliographic Reviews of Far Eastern Archaeology 1990.* Oxford: Oxbow, pp. 63–111.

Hudson, M. J. (1992). Rice, bronze and chieftains: an archaeology of Yayoi ritual. *Japanese Journal of Religious Studies,* 19 (2–3), 139–89 (https://nirc .nanzan-u.ac.jp/nfile/2487).

Hudson, M. J. (1999). *Ruins of Identity: Ethnogenesis in the Japanese Islands.* Honolulu: University of Hawai'i Press.

Hudson, M. J. (2004). The perverse realities of change: world system incorporation and the Okhotsk culture of Hokkaido. *Journal of Anthropological Archaeology,* 23, 290–308.

Hudson, M. J. (2019). Towards a prehistory of the Great Divergence: the Bronze Age roots of Japan's premodern economy. *Documenta Praehistorica,* 46, 30–43.

Hudson, M. J. (2020a). Language dispersals and the 'secondary peoples' revolution': a historical anthropology of the Transeurasian unity. In M. Robbeets and A. Savelyev, eds., *The Oxford Guide to the Transeurasian Languages.* Oxford: Oxford University Press, pp. 806–13.

Hudson, M. J. (2020b). Slouching toward the Neolithic: complexity, simplification and resilience in the Japanese archipelago. In G. R. Schug, ed., *The Routledge Handbook of the Bioarchaelogy of Climate and Environmental Change.* London: Routledge, pp. 379–95.

Hudson. M. J. (2021a). Dragon divers and clamorous fishermen: Bronzisation and transcultural marine spaces in the Japanese archipelago. In S. Autiero and M. A. Cobb, eds., *Globalization and Transculturality from Antiquity to the Pre-modern World.* London: Routledge, pp. 103–19.

Hudson, M. J. (2021b). *Conjuring Up Prehistory: Landscape and the Archaic in Japanese Nationalism.* Oxford: Archaeopress.

Hudson, M. J. (in press). Globalisation and the historical evolution of Japanese fisheries. In J. Cassidy, I. Ponkratova and B. Fitzhugh, eds., *Maritime Prehistory of Northeast Asia.* New York: Springer.

Hudson, M. J., & Barnes, G. L. (1991). Yoshinogari: a Yayoi settlement in northern Kyushu. *Monumenta Nipponica,* 46(2), 211–35.

Hudson, M.J., Bausch, I. R., Robbeets, M., Li, T., White, J. A. & Gilaizeau, L. (2021). Bronze Age globalisation and later Jōmon social change. *Journal of World Prehistory,* 34, 121–58.

Hudson, M. J., & Robbeets, M. (2020). Archaeolinguistic evidence for the farming/ language dispersal of Koreanic. *Evolutionary Human Sciences,* 2, e52.

Hudson, M. J., Schulting, R. J. & Gilaizeau, L. (2020). The origins of violence and warfare in the Japanese islands. In G. G. Fagan, L. Fibiger, M. J. Hudson and M. Trundle, eds., *The Cambridge World History of Violence, Volume 1: The Prehistoric and Ancient Worlds*. Cambridge: Cambridge University Press, pp. 160–77.

Hung, H.-C., & Chao, C.-Y. (2016). Taiwan's Early Metal Age and Southeast Asian trading systems. *Antiquity*, 90, 1537–51.

Hung, H.-C., Iizuka, Y., Bellwood, P., Nguyen, K. D., Bellina, B., Silapanth, P., Dizon, E., Santiago, R., Datan, I. & Manton, J. H. (2007). Ancient jades map 3,000 years of prehistoric exchange in Southeast Asia. *Proceedings of the National Academy of Sciences USA*, 104(50), 19745–50.

Ialongo, N. (2018). The earliest balance weights in the west: towards an independent metrology for Bronze Age Europe. *Cambridge Archaeological Journal*, 29, 103–24.

Imamura, K. (1996). *Prehistoric Japan: New Perspectives on Insular East Asia*. London: UCL Press.

Isomae, J. (2002). The space of historical discourse: Ishimoda Shō's theory of the Heroic Age. *Positions*, 10(3), 631–68.

Iwanaga, S. (2018). Interaction between the Korean peninsula and the Japanese archipelago during the Yayoi period. In M. E. Byington, K. Sasaki & M. T. Bale, eds., *Early Korea–Japan Interactions*. Cambridge, MA: Korea Institute, Harvard University, pp. 91–131.

Jaffe, Y. Y., & Flad, R. (2018). Prehistoric globalizing processes in the Tao river valley, Gansu, China? In N. Boivin & M. Frachetti, eds., *Globalization in Prehistory: Contact, Exchange, and the 'People without History'*. Cambridge: Cambridge University Press, pp. 131–61.

Jaffe, Y. Y., & Hein, A. (2021). Considering change with archaeological data: reevaluating local variation in the role of the ~4.2 k BP event in northwest China. *Holocene*, 31, 169–82.

Jennings, J. (2016). *Killing Civilization: A Reassessment of Early Urbanism and Its Consequences*. Albuquerque: University of New Mexico Press.

Jeong, C. Wilkin, S., Amgalantugs, T. (2018). Bronze Age population dynamics and the rise of dairy pastoralism on the eastern Eurasian steppe. *Proceedings of the National Academy of Sciences USA*, 115(48), e11248–e11255.

Jeong, C. Wang, K., Wilkin, S. et al. (2020). A dynamic 6000-year genetic history of Eurasia's eastern steppe. *Cell*, 183, 890–904.

Jervis, B. (2017). Assembling the archaeology of the global Middle Ages. *World Archaeology*, 49, 666–80.

Kameda, S. (2018). Ancient Kibi, western Japan, and the Korean peninsula. In M. E. Byington, K. Sasaki & M. T. Bale, eds., *Early Korea–Japan Interactions*. Cambridge, MA: Korea Institute, Harvard University, pp. 231–70.

Kamberov, Y. G., Wang, S., Tan, J. et al. (2013). Modeling recent human evolution in mice by expression of a selected EDAR variant. *Cell*, 152, 691–702.

Kaner, S. (2011). The archaeology of religion and ritual in the prehistoric Japanese archipelago. In T. Insoll, ed., *Oxford Handbook of the Archaeology of Ritual and Religion*. Oxford: Oxford University Press, pp. 457–69.

Kanzawa-Kiriyama, H. Kryukov, K., Jinam, T. A. et al. (2017). A partial nuclear genome of the Jomons who lived 3000 years ago in Fukushima, Japan. *Journal of Human Genetics*, 62, 213–21.

Kawashima, T. (2015). Prehistoric salt production in Japan. In R. Brigand and O. Weller, eds., *Archaeology of Salt: Approaching an Invisible Past*. Leiden: Sidestone Press, pp. 125–38.

Keightley, D. (1993). Clean hands and shining helmets: heroic action in early China and Greek culture. In T. Siebers, ed., *Religion and the Authority of the Past*. Ann Arbor: University of Michigan Press, pp. 253–81.

Kidder, J. E. (1995). Problems of Jomon population decline. In ICU Archaeology Research Center, ed., *Nogawa Site (1)*. Tokyo: International Christian University, pp. 105–10.

Kidder, J. E. (2007). *Himiko and Japan's Elusive Chiefdom of Yamatai: Archaeology, History, and Mythology*. Honolulu: University of Hawai'i Press.

Kikuchi, T. (2004). *Kan-Ohōtsukukai kodai bunka no kenkyū [A Study of the Ancient Cultures around the Sea of Okhotsk]*. Sapporo: Hokkaido University Press.

Kinoshita, N. (2019a). Prehistoric Ryūkyūan seafaring: a cultural and environmental perspective. In C. Wu and B. V. Rolett, eds., *Prehistoric Maritime Cultures and Seafaring in East Asia*. New York: Springer, pp. 315–32.

Kinoshita, N. (2019b). Nantō senshi bunka to Jōmon, Yayoi bunka: Okinawa no kaizuka bunka o chūshin ni [The prehistoric cultures of the southern islands and Jōmon and Yayoi cultures: with special reference to the Shellmound culture of Okinawa]. In National Museum of Japanese History and S. Fujio, eds., *Saikō! Jōmon to Yayoi: Nihon senshi bunka no saikōchiku [Reconsidering Jōmon and Yayoi: Restructuring the Prehistoric Cultures of Japan]*. Yoshikawa Kōbunkan, pp. 10–39.

Kitajima, D. (2019). Seidōki no matsuri to wa nani ka [What were bronze festivals?]. In Y. Hōjō, ed., *Kōkogaku kōgi [Archaeology Lectures]*. Chikuma Shobō.

Kobayashi, S. (2014). Bronze cultures around eastern Eurasia at 1st millennium BC and the origin of Yayoi bronzeware. *Bulletin of the National Museum of Japanese History*, 185, 213–38 (in Japanese with English summary).

Kobayashi, S. (2017). *Wajin no saishi kōkogaku* [*The Ritual Archaeology of the Wa*]. Shinsensha.

Koyama, S. (1978). Jomon subsistence and population. *Senri Ethnological Studies*, 2, 1–65.

Kristiansen, K. (1998). *Europe before History*. Cambridge: Cambridge University Press.

Kristiansen, K. (1999). The emergence of warrior aristocracies in later European prehistory. In J. Carman & A. Harding, eds., *Ancient Warfare: Archaeological Perspectives*. Stroud: Sutton Publishing, pp. 175–189.

Kristiansen, K. (2006). Eurasian transformations: mobility, ecological change, and the transmission of social institutions in the third millennium and the early second millennium BCE. In A. Hornborg & C. Crumley, eds., *The World System and the Earth System: Global Socioenvironmental Change and Sustainability since the Neolithic*. Walnut Creek, CA: Left Coast Press, pp. 149–62.

Kristiansen, K. (2015). The decline of the Neolithic and the rise of Bronze Age society. In C. Fowler, J. Harding and D. Hofman, eds., *The Oxford Handbook of Neolithic Europe*. Oxford: Oxford University Press, pp. 1093–1117.

Kristiansen, K. (2018). The rise of Bronze Age peripheries and the expansion of international trade 1950–1100 BC. In K. Kristiansen, T. Linkvist & J. Myrdal, eds., *Trade and Civilisation: Economic Networks and Cultural Ties, from Prehistory to the Early Modern Era*. Cambridge: Cambridge University Press, pp. 87–112.

Kristiansen, K., & Larsson, T. B. (2005). *The Rise of Bronze Age Society: Travels, Transmissions and Transformations*. Cambridge: Cambridge University Press.

Kuwabara, H. (1995). Yayoi jidai ni okeru seidōki no fukusō to mainō [Bronze burials and hoards in the Yayoi period]. In Nishitani Shinji sensei no koki o oiwai suru kai, eds., *Nishitani Shinji sensei koki kinen ronbunshū* [*Festschrift for the 70th Birthday of Professor Shinji Nishitani*]. Benseisha, pp. 15–47.

Lattimore, O. (1962). *Studies in Frontier History: Collected Papers, 1928–1958*. Oxford: Oxford University Press.

Laufer, B. (1913). Arabic and Chinese trade in walrus and narwhal ivory. *T'oung Pao*, 14, 315–70.

Ledyard, G. (1975). Galloping along with the Horseriders: looking for the founders of Japan. *Journal of Japanese Studies*, 1, 217–54.

Lee, G.-A. (2017). The spread of domesticated plant resources in prehistoric northeast Asia. In T. Hodos, ed., *The Routledge Handbook of Archaeology and Globalization*. London: Routledge, pp. 394–412.

Li, T., Ning, C., Zhushchikhovskaya, I. S., Hudson, M. J. & Robbeets, M. (2020). Millet agriculture dispersed from northeast China to the Russian Far East: integrating archaeology, genetics and linguistics. *Archaeological Research in Asia*, 22, e100177.

Linduff, K., & Mei, J. (2009). Metallurgy in ancient eastern Asia: retrospect and prospects. *Journal of World Prehistory*, 22, 265–81.

Linduff, K., Sun, Y., Cao, W. & Liu, Y. (2018). *Ancient China and Its Eurasian Neighbors: Artifacts, Identity and Death in the Frontier, 3000–700 BCE.* Cambridge: Cambridge University Press.

Ling, J., & Cornell, P. (2017). Violence, warriors, and rock art in Bronze Age Scandinavia. In R. J. Chacon and R. G. Mendoza, eds., *Feast, Famine or Fighting? Multiple Pathways to Social Complexity.* New York: Springer, pp. 15–33.

Ling, J., Earle, T. & Kristiansen, K. (2018). Maritime mode of production: raiding and trading in seafaring chiefdoms. *Current Anthropology*, 59, 488–524.

Ling, J., & Toreld, A. (2018). Maritime warfare in Scandinavian rock art. In C. Horn and K. Kristiansen, eds., *Warfare in Bronze Age Society.* Cambridge: Cambridge University Press, pp. 61–80.

Littleton, C. S. (1995). Yamato-takeru: an 'Arthurian' hero in Japanese tradition. *Asian Folklore Studies*, 54, 259–74.

Liu, L., & Chen, X. (2012). *The Archaeology of Ancient China: From the Late Paleolithic to the Early Bronze Age.* Cambridge: Cambridge University Press.

Liu, S., Chen, K. L., Rehren, T., Mei, J. J., Chen, J. L., Liu, Y. & Killick, D. (2018). Did China import metals from Africa in the Bronze Age? *Archaeometry*, 60, 105–17.

Liu, X., Jones, P. J., Matuzeviciute, G. M., Hunt, H. V., Lister, D. L., An, T., Przelomska, N., Kneale, C. J., Zhao, Z. & Jones, M. K. (2019). From ecological opportunism to multi-cropping: mapping food globalisation in prehistory. *Quaternary Science Reviews*, 206, 21–8.

Long, T., Leipe, C., Jin, G., Wagner, M., Guo, R., Schröder, O. & Tarasov, P.E. (2018). The early history of wheat in China from 14 C dating and Bayesian chronological modelling. *Nature Plants*, 4, 272–9.

Long, T., Wagner, M., Demske, D., Leipe, C. & Tarasov, P. E. (2017). Cannabis in Eurasia: origin of human use and Bronze Age trans-continental connections. *Vegetation History and Archaeobotany*, 26, 245–58.

Ma, T., Rolett, B. V., Zheng, Z. & Zong, Y. (2020). Holocene coastal evolution preceded the expansion of paddy field rice farming. *Proceedings of the National Academy of Sciences USA*, 117(39), 24138–43.

Maringer, J. (1974). Clay figurines of the Jōmon period: a contribution to the history of ancient religion in Japan. *History of Religions*, 14, 128–39.

Maringer, J. (1979). Adorants in prehistoric art: prehistoric attitudes and gestures of prayer. *Numen*, 26, 215–30.

Mason, O. K. (2009). 'The multiplication of forms': Bering Strait harpoon heads as a demic and macroevolutionary proxy. In A.M. Prentiss, I. Kuijy & J.C. Chatters, eds., *Macroevolution in Human Prehistory: Evolutionary Theory and Processual Archaeology*. New York: Springer, pp. 73–107.

Mason, O. K., & Rasic, J. T. (2019). Walrusing, whaling and the origins of the Old Bering Sea culture. *World Archaeology*, 51, 454–83.

Matsugi, T. (2001). *Hito wa naze tatakau no ka? Kōkogaku kara mita sensō* [*Why do Humans Fight? War Seen from Archaeology*]. Kōdansha.

Matsugi, T. (2018). The development of metalworking and the formation of political power in the Japanese archipelago. In T. Knopf, W. Steinhaus & S. Fukunaga, eds., *Burial Mounds in Europe and Japan: Comparative and Contextual Perspectives*. Oxford: Archaeopress, pp. 173–81.

Matsumoto, K. (2021). The Bronze Age in the Eurasian steppes. *Japanese Journal of Archaeology*, 8, 287–328.

Matsushita, T. (1994). *Nihonjin to Yayoijin: sono nazo no ruutsu o keishitsu jinruigaku ga akasu.* [*The Japanese and the Yayoi People: Physical Anthropology Illuminates Their Mysterious Roots*]. Shōdensha.

Miyamoto, K. (2018). A new discussion of the actual date of the beginning of the Yayoi period. *Kōkogaku Zasshi*, 100, 1–27 (in Japanese with English summary).

Miyamoto, K. (2019). The spread of rice agriculture during the Yayoi period: from the Shandong peninsula to the Japanese archipelago via the Korean peninsula. *Japanese Journal of Archaeology*, 6, 109–24.

Mizoguchi, K. (2013). *The Archaeology of Japan: From the Earliest Rice Farming Villages to the Rise of the State*. Cambridge: Cambridge University Press.

Mödlinger, M. (2017). *Protecting the Body in War and Combat: Metal Body Armour in Bronze Age Europe*. Vienna: Austrian Academy of Sciences Press.

Molloy, B. (2017). Hunting warriors: the transformation of weapons, combat practices and society during the Bronze Age in Ireland. *European Journal of Archaeology*, 20, 280–316.

Molloy, B., & Horn, C. (2020). Weapons, warriors and warfare in Bronze Age Europe. In G. G. Fagan, L. Fibiger, M. J. Hudson & M. Trundle, eds., *The Cambridge World History of Violence, Volume 1: The Prehistoric and Ancient Worlds*. Cambridge: Cambridge University Press, pp. 117–41.

Morimoto, S. (2012). Yayoi jidai no bundō [Weights of the Yayoi period]. *Kōkogaku Kenkyū*, 59, 67–75.

Morris-Suzuki, T. (1993). Rewriting history: civilization theory in contemporary Japan. *Positions: East Asia Cultures Critique*, 1, 526–49.

Müller, J. (2013). Demographic traces of technological innovation, social change and mobility: from 1 to 8 million Europeans (6000–2000 BCE). In S. Kradow & P. Włodarczak, eds., *Environment and Subsistence: Forty Years after Janusz Kruk's 'Settlement Studies'*. Rzeszów & Bonn: Mitel & Verlag, pp. 1–14.

Nagahara, K., & Yamamura, K. (1988). Shaping the process of unification: technological progress in sixteenth- and seventeenth-century Japan. *Journal of Japanese Studies*, 14, 77–109.

Nakagawa, T., Nakao, H., Tamura, K., Arimatsu, Y., Matsumoto, N. & Matsugi, T. (2017). Violence and warfare in prehistoric Japan. *Letters on Evolutionary Behavioral Science*, 8, 8–11.

Nakajima, T., Hudson, M., Uchiyama, J., Makibayashi, K. & Zhang, J. (2019). Common carp aquaculture in Neolithic China dates back 8000 years. *Nature Ecology & Evolution*, 3, 1415–18.

Nakao, H., Tamura, K., Arimatsu, Y., Nakagawa, T., Matsumoto, N. & Matsugi, T. (2016). Violence in the prehistoric period of Japan: the spatio-temporal pattern of skeletal evidence for violence in the Jomon period. *Biology Letters*, 12, e20160028.

Nakazono, S. (2011). The role of long-distance interaction in sociocultural changes in the Yayoi period, Japan. In N. Matsumoto, H. Bessho & M. Tomii, eds., *Coexistence and Cultural Transmission in East Asia*. Walnut Creek, CA: Left Coast Press, pp. 49–67.

Nanba, Y. (2016). Dōtaku no kakaku [The price of bronze bells]. *Kikan Kōkogaku*, 135, 70–4.

Nasu, H., Gu, H., Momohara, A. & Yasuda, Y. (2012). Land-use change for rice and foxtail millet cultivation in the Chengtoushan site, central China, reconstructed from weed seed assemblages. *Archaeological and Anthropological Sciences*, 4, 1–14.

Nelson, S. (1999). Megalithic monuments and the introduction of rice into Korea. In C. Gosden & J. Hather, eds., *The Prehistory of Food: Appetites for Change*. London: Routledge, pp. 147–65.

Ning, C. Li, T., Wang, K. et al. (2020). Ancient genomes from northern China suggest links between subsistence changes and human migration. *Nature Communications*, 11, e2700.

Ōbayashi, T. (1975). *Shinwa to shinwagaku [Myths and Mythology]*. Yamato Shobō.

Oda, S. (1990). A review of archaeological research in the Izu and Ogasawara islands. *Man & Culture in Oceania*, 6, 53–79.

Oh, Y., Conte, M., Kang, S., Kim, J. & Hwang, J. (2017). Population fluctuation and the adoption of food production in prehistoric Korea: using radiocarbon dates as a proxy for population change. *Radiocarbon*, 59, 1761–70.

Oikawa, A. & Koyama, S. (1981). A Jomon shellmound database. *Senri Ethnological Studies*, 9, 187–99.

Oliveira, N. V., O'Connor, S. & Bellwood, P. (2019). Dong Son drums from Timor-Leste: prehistoric bronze artefacts in Island Southeast Asia. *Antiquity*, 93, 163–80.

Pailler, Y. et al. (2019). Beg ar Loued, Molène island, Finistère (France), an Early Bronze Age insular settlement: between autarchy and openness to the outside world. In H. Meller, S. Friedriech, M. Küßner, H. Stäuble & R. Risch, eds., *Siedlungsarchäologie des Endneolithikums und der frühen Bronzezeit – Late Neolithic and Early Bronze Age Settlement Archaeology*. Halle: Landesamt für Denkmalpflege und Archäologie Sachsen-Anhalt, pp. 949–85.

Palmer, E. (2015). *Harima Fudoki: A Record of Ancient Japan Reinterpreted, Translated, Annotated, and with Commentary*. Leiden: Brill.

Park, C. S. (2018). Kaya, Silla, and Wa: changing relationships and their historical backgrounds. In M.E. Byington, K. Sasaki & M.T. Bale, eds., *Early Korea-Japan Interactions*. Cambridge MA: Early Korea Project, Korea Institute, Harvard University, pp. 133–181.

Pearson, R. (1990). Chiefly exchange between Kyushu and Okinawa, Japan, in the Yayoi period. *Antiquity*, 64, 912–22.

Pearson, R. (2006). Jomon hot spot: increasing sedentism in south-western Japan in the Incipient Jomon (14,000–9250 cal. BC) and Earliest Jomon (9250–5300 cal. BC) periods. *World Archaeology*, 38(2), 239–58.

Pearson, R. (2013). *Ancient Ryukyu: An Archaeological Study of Island Communities*. Honolulu: University of Hawai'i Press.

Pellard, T. (2015). The linguistic archaeology of the Ryukyu Islands. In P. Heinrich, S. Miyara & M. Shimoji, eds., *Handbook of the Ryukyu Languages: History, Structure and Use*. Berlin: de Gruyter, pp. 13–37.

Philippi, D. L. (1969). *Kojiki*. University of Tokyo Press.

Piggott, J. (1989). Sacral kingship and confederacy in early Izumo. *Monumenta Nipponica*, 44(1), 45–74.

Pinker, S. (2011). *The Better Angels of Our Nature: A History of Violence and Humanity*. New York: Penguin.

Popov, A. N., Zhushchikhovskaya, I. S. & Nikitin, Y.G. (2019). Paleometal epoch in the Primorye (south of the Far East of Russia). *World Archaeology*, 51, 382–407.

Price, T. D., Frei, R., Brinker, U., Lidke, G., Terberger, T., Frei, K. M. & Jantzen, D. (2019). Multi-isotope proveniencing of human remains from a Bronze Age battlefield in the Tollense valley in northeast Germany. *Archaeological and Anthropological Sciences*, 11, 33–49.

Qin, L., & Fuller, D.Q. (2019). Why rice farmers don't sail: coastal subsistence traditions and maritime trends in early China. In C. Wu and B. V. Rolett, eds., *Prehistoric Maritime Cultures and Seafaring in East Asia*. New York: Springer, pp. 159–91.

Rahmstorf, L. (2019). Scales, weights and weight-regulated artefacts in Middle and Late Bronze Age Britain. *Antiquity*, 93, 1197–1210.

Rascovan, N., Sjögren, K.-G., Kristiansen, K., Nielsen, R., Willerslev, E., Desnues, C. & Rasmussen, S. (2019). Emergence and spread of basal lineages of *Yersinia pestis* during the Neolithic decline. *Cell*, 176, 1–11.

Ratnagar, S. (2001). The Bronze Age: unique instance of a pre-industrial world system? *Current Anthropology*, 42(3), 351–79.

Rawson, J. (2015). Steppe weapons in ancient China and the role of hand-to-hand combat. *National Palace Museum Research Quarterly*, 33(1), 37–95.

Rawson, J. (2017). China and the steppe: reception and resistance. *Antiquity*, 91, 375–88.

Ren, G. Zhang, X., Li, Y. et al. (2021). Large-scale whole-genome resequencing unravels the domestication history of *Cannabis sativa*. *Science Advances*, 7, eabg2286.

Rhee, S.-N., Aikens, C. M., Choi, S.-R. & Ro, H.-J. (2007). Korean contributions to agriculture, technology, and state formation in Japan: archaeology and history of an epochal thousand years, 400 BC–AD 600. *Asian Perspectives*, 46(2), 404–59.

Richards, M. P., Schulting, R. J. & Hedges, R. E. M. (2003) Sharp shift in diet at onset of Neolithic. *Nature*, 425, 366.

Robbeets, M., Bouckaert, R., Conte, M. et al. (2021). Triangulation supports agricultural spread of the Transeurasian languages. *Nature*, 599, 616–621.

Rolett, B. V., Zheng, Z. & Yue, Y. (2011). Holocene sea-level change and the emergence of Neolithic seafaring in the Fuzhou basin (Fujian, China). *Quaternary Science Reviews*, 30, 788–97.

Rowlands, M. & Fuller, D. Q. (2018). Deconstructing civilisation: a 'Neolithic' alternative. In K. Kristiansen, T. Lindkvist & J. Myrdal, eds., *Trade and Civilisation: Economic Networks and Cultural Ties, from Prehistory to the Early Modern Era*. Cambridge: Cambridge University Press, pp. 172–94.

Rowley-Conwy, P. & Layton, R. (2011). Foraging and farming as niche construction: stable and unstable adaptations. *Philosophical Transactions of the Royal Society B*, 366, 849–62.

Ryan, J., & Barnes, G. (2014). Armor in Japan and Korea. In S. Helaine, ed., *Encyclopaedia of the History of Science, Technology and Medicine in Non-Western Cultures*. New York: Springer, pp. 1–16.

Sabatini, S., & Bergerbrant, S., eds. (2020). *The Textile Revolution in Bronze Age Europe: Production, Specialisation, Consumption*. Cambridge: Cambridge University Press.

Sahara, M. (1987a). *Nihonjin no tanjō* [*The Birth of the Japanese*]. Shōgakukan.

Sahara, M. (1987b). The Yayoi culture. In K. Tsuboi, ed., *Recent Archaeological Discoveries in Japan*. Paris: UNESCO, pp. 37–54.

Sanft, C. (2020). Violence in early Chinese history. In G. G. Fagan, L. Fibiger, M. J. Hudson & M. Trundle, eds., *The Cambridge World History of Violence, Volume 1: The Prehistoric and Ancient Worlds*. Cambridge: Cambridge University Press, pp. 418–37.

Sansom, G. B. (1924). The imperial edicts in the Shoku Nihongi (700–790 AD). *Transactions of the Asiatic Society of Japan*, 2nd series, 1, 5–39.

Sasaki, K. (2017). The Kofun era and early state formation. In K. F. Friday, ed., *Routledge Handbook of Premodern Japanese History*. London: Routledge, pp. 68–81.

Sasaki, K. (2018). Adoption of the practice of horse-riding in Kofun period Japan: with special reference to the case of the central highlands of Japan. *Japanese Journal of Archaeology*, 6, 23–53.

Schafer, E. H. (1989). Fusang and beyond: the haunted seas to Japan. *Journal of the American Oriental Society*, 109(3), 379–99.

Schroeder, H. Margaryan, A., Szmyt, M. et al. (2019). Unraveling ancestry, kinship, and violence in a Late Neolithic mass grave. *Proceedings of the National Academy of Sciences USA*, 116(22), 10705–10.

Schulting, R. J. (2013). War without warriors? The nature of interpersonal conflict before the emergence of formalized warrior elites. In S. Ralph, ed., *The Archaeology of Violence: Interdisciplinary Approaches*. Albany: SUNY Press, pp. 19–36.

Schulting, R. & Fibiger, L., eds. (2012). *Sticks, Stones and Broken Bones: Neolithic Violence in a European Perspective*. Oxford: Oxford University Press.

Scott, J. C. (2009). *The Art of Not Being Governed: An Anarchist History of Upland Southeast Asia*. New Haven, CT: Yale University Press.

Scott, J. C. (2017). *Against the Grain: A Deep History of the Earliest States*. New Haven, CT: Yale University Press.

Scott, J. C. (2019). Response. *Cambridge Archaeological Journal*, 29, 716–21.

Seeley, C. (1991). *A History of Writing in Japan*. Leiden: Brill.

Segawa, T. (2017). *Jōmon no shisō* [*The Thought of the Jōmon*]. Kōdansha.

Sekine, T. (2014). Changes in the number of archaeological sites during the Jomon period in Aomori Prefecture, northeastern Japan. *Daiyonki Kenkyū (The Quaternary Research)*, 53 (4), 193–203(in Japanese with English summary).

Seyock, B. (2003). The culture of Han and Wa around the Korean straits: an archaeological perspective. *Acta Koreana*, 6, 63–86.

Seyock, B. (2004). *Auf den Spuren der Ostbarbaren: Zur Archäologie proto-historischer Kulturen in Südkorea und Westjapan*. Münster: Lit.

Shaughnessy, E. L. (1988). Historical perspectives on the introduction of the chariot into China. *Harvard Journal of Asiatic Studies*, 48, 189–237.

Shelach-Lavi, G. (2015). *The Archaeology of Early China: From Prehistory to the Han Dynasty*. Cambridge: Cambridge University Press.

Shelach-Lavi, G., Teng, M., Goldsmith, Y., Wachtel, I., Stevens, C. J., Marder, O., Wan, X., Wu, X., Tu, D., Shavit, R., Polissar, P., Xu, H. & Fuller, D. Q. (2019). Sedentism and plant cultivation in northeast China emerged during affluent conditions. *PLoS ONE*, 14(7), e0218751.

Shennan, S., Downey, S. S., Timpson, A., Edinborough, K., Colledge, S., Kerig, T., Manning, K. & Thomas, M. G. (2013). Regional population collapse followed initial agriculture booms in mid-Holocene Europe. *Nature Communications*, 4, 2486.

Sherratt, A. (1981). Plough and pastoralism: aspects of the secondary products revolution. In I. Hodder, G. Isaac and N. Hammond, eds., *Pattern of the Past: Studies in Honour of David Clarke*. Cambridge: Cambridge University Press, pp. 261–305.

Sherratt, A. (1993). What would a Bronze-Age world system look like? Relations between temperate Europe and the Mediterranean in later prehistory. *Journal of European Archaeology*, 1(2), 1–37.

Sherratt, A. (2011). Global development. In T. C. Wilkinson, S. Sherratt & J. Bennet, eds., *Interweaving Worlds: Systemic Interactions in Eurasia, 7th to 1st Millennia BC*. Oxford: Oxbow, pp. 4–6.

Shimane Board of Education (1996). *Izumo Kanba Kōjindani iseki [The Kanba Kōjindani Site, Izumo]*. Matsue: Shimane Prefecture.

Shintani, T., & Okada, Y. (1986). Aomori-ken Tairadate-son Imazu iseki shut-sudo no jōsansoku doki [The three-legged pot excavated from the Imazu site, Tairadate village, Aomori prefecture]. *Kōkogaku Zasshi*, 71, 241–6.

Shinzato, T. (2018). Kaizuka jidai kō 1 ki no doki bunka [The ceramic culture of the Late 1 phase of the Shellmound period]. In H. Takamiya, ed., *Amami, Okinawa shotō senshigaku no saizensen [The Frontier of the Prehistory of the Amami and Okinawa Archipelagos]*. Kagoshima: Nanpō Shinsha, pp. 20–44.

Shitara, H. (2014a). The origin of *dotaku* design. *Bulletin of the Department of Archaeology, University of Tokyo*, 28, 109–30 (in Japanese with English summary).

Shitara, H. (2014b). *Jōmon shakai to Yayoi shakai* [Jōmon Society and Yayoi Society]. Keibunsha.

Shitara, H. (2018). Consideration to [*sic*] Obara-type pottery at the end of the Jomon period in *Nansei-shoto*. *Bulletin of the Department of Archaeology, University of Tokyo*, 31, 47–60 (in Japanese with English summary).

Sim, R., & Wallis, L. A. (2008). Northern Australian offshore island use during the Holocene: the archaeology of Vanderlin Island, Sir Edward Pellew Group, Gulf of Carpentaria. *Australian Archaeology*, 67, 95–106.

Skoda, H. (2013). *Medieval Violence: Physical Brutality in Northern France, 1270–1330*. Oxford: Oxford University Press.

Smits, G. (2019). *Maritime Ryukyu, 1050–1650*. Honolulu: University of Hawai'i Press.

Sofaer, J., Jørgensen, L. B. & Choyke, A. (2013). Craft production: ceramics, textiles, and bone. In H. Fokkens & A. Harding, eds., *The Oxford Handbook of the European Bronze Age*. Oxford: Oxford University Press, pp. 469–91.

Spengler, R. N. (2019). *Fruit From the Sands: The Silk Road Origins of the Foods We Eat*. Berkeley: University of California Press.

Spriggs, M. (2018). Elliot Smith reborn? A view of prehistoric globalization from the Island Southeast Asian and Pacific margins. In K. Kristiansen, T. Lindkvist & J. Myrdal, eds., *Trade and Civilisation: Economic Networks and Cultural Ties, from Prehistory to the Early Modern Era*. Cambridge: Cambridge University Press, pp. 410–40.

Stevens, C. J., & Fuller, D. Q. (2012). Did Neolithic farming fail? The case for a Bronze Age agricultural revolution in the British Isles. *Antiquity*, 86, 707–22.

Stevens, C. J., & Fuller, D.Q. (2017). The spread of agriculture in eastern Asia: archaeological bases for hypothetical farmer/language dispersals. *Language Dynamics and Change*, 7, 152–86.

Storozum, M. J., Qin, Z., Wang, Y. V. & Liu, H. (2020). Buried soils as archives of paleo-pollution in the North China Plain. *Anthropocene*, 31, e100251.

Sugiyama, K. (2014). *Yayoi bunka to kaijin* [*Yayoi Culture and Sea Peoples*]. Rokuichi Shobō.

Sun, W., Zhang, L., Guo, J., Li, C., Jiang, Y., Zartman, R. & Zhang, Z. (2016). Origin of the mysterious Yin-Shang bronzes in China indicated by lead isotopes. *Scientific Reports*, 6, e23304.

Szczesniak, B. (1951). The Kōtaiō monument. *Monumenta Nipponica*, 7, 242–68.

Takamiya, H. (2001). Introductory routes of rice to Japan: an examination of the southern route hypothesis. *Asian Perspectives*, 40(2), 209–26.

Takamiya, H., Hudson, M., Yonenobu, H., Kurozumi, T. & Toizumi, T. (2016). An extraordinary case in human history: prehistoric hunter-gatherer adaptation to the islands of the central Ryukyus (Okinawa and Amami archipelagos), Japan. *Holocene*, 26(3), 408–22.

Takase, K. (2017). 'Michinoku no Ongagawa' saikō [A reconsideration of the 'Michinoku Ongagawa']. *Kikan Kōkogaku*, 138, 59–62.

Takase, K. (2019). Long-term marine resource use in Hokkaido, northern Japan: new insights into sea mammal hunting and fishing. *World Archaeology*, 51(3), 408–28.

Takesue, J. (2009). Interaction between the Three Han states and Wa: from the perspective of settlements based on marine resources. *Bulletin of the National Museum of Japanese History*, 151, 285–306 (in Japanese with English summary).

Tanaka, M. (1991). *Nihon no rekishi 2: Wajin sōran* [*History of Japan 2: The Wa Unrest*]. Shūeisha.

Taylor, W. T. T., Bayarsaikhan, J. & Tuvshinjargal, T. (2015). Equine cranial morphology and the identification of riding and chariotry in late Bronze Age Mongolia. *Antiquity*, 89, 854–71.

Teramae, N. (2017). *Bunmei ni kōshita Yayoi no hitobito* [*The Yayoi People's Resistance to Civilisation*]. Yoshikawa Kōbunkan.

Terasawa, K. (2000). *Ōken tanjō* [*The Birth of Royal Power*]. Kōdansha.

Tezuka, K. (1998). Long-distance trade networks and shipping in the Ezo region. *Arctic Anthropology*, 35, 350–60.

Toizumi, T. (2018). Okinawa no jūnikushoku [Meat-eating in Okinawa]. *Kikan Kōkogaku*, 144, 63–4.

Torrance, R. (2016). The infrastructure of the gods: Izumo in the Yayoi and Kofun periods. *Japan Review*, 29, 3–38.

Treherne, P. (1995). The warrior's beauty: the masculine body and self-identity in Bronze-Age Europe. *Journal of European Archaeology*, 3, 105–44.

Tsunoda, R., & Goodrich, L. C. (1951). *Japan in the Chinese Dynastic Histories: Later Han through Ming Dynasties*. South Pasadena, CA: P.D. & Ione Perkins.

Uchiyama, J., Gillam, J. C., Savelyev, A. & Ning, C. (2020). Populations [*sic*] dynamics in northern Eurasian forests: a long-term perspective from Northeast Asia. *Evolutionary Human Sciences*, 2, e16.

Uhlig, T., Krüger, J., Lidke, G., Jantzen, D., Lorenz, S., Ialongo, N. & Terberger, T. (2019). Lost in combat? A scrap metal find from the Bronze Age battlefield site at Tollense. *Antiquity*, 93, 1211–30.

Vandkilde, H. (2006) Warfare and gender according to Homer: an archaeology of an aristocratic warrior culture. In T. Otto, H. Thrane & H. Vandkilde, eds., *Warfare and Society: Archaeological and Social Anthropological Perspectives*. Aarhus: Aarhus University Press, pp. 515–528.

Vandkilde, H. (2014). Breakthrough of the Nordic Bronze Age: transcultural warriorhood and a Carpathian crossroad in the sixteenth century BC. *European Journal of Archaeology*, 17(4), 602–33.

Vandkilde, H. (2016). Bronzization: the Bronze Age as pre-modern globalization. *Praehistorische Zeitschrift*, 91, 103–23.

Vandkilde, H. (2019). Bronze Age beginnings: a scalar view from the global outskirts. *Proceedings of the Prehistoric Society*, 85, 1–27.

von Falkenhausen, L. (2006). The salt of Ba: reflections on the role of the 'peripheries' in the production systems of Bronze Age China. *Arts Asiatiques*, 61, 45–56.

von Falkenhausen, L. (2008). Stages in the development of 'cities' in pre-imperial China. In J. Marcus & J. A. Sabloff, eds., *Ancient City: New Perspectives on Urbanism in the Old and New World*. Santa Fe, NM: School for Advanced Research, pp. 209–28.

von Verschuer, C. (2006). *Across the Perilous Sea: Japanese Trade with China and Korea from the Seventh to the Sixteenth Centuries*. Ithaca, NY: East Asia Program, Cornell University. Originally published in 1988 as *Le Commerce extérieur du Japon des origines aux XVIe siècle* (Paris: Collège de France).

Wagner, M., & Tarasov, P. (2014). The Neolithic of northern and central China. In C. Renfrew & P. Bahn, eds., *The Cambridge World Prehistory. Vol. 2: East Asia and the Americas*. Cambridge: Cambridge University Press, pp. 742–64.

Wang, C.-C. Yeh, H-Y., Popov, A. N. et al. (2021). Genomic insights into the formation of human populations in East Asia. *Nature*, 591, 413–19.

Wang, Z. (2005). *Ambassadors from the Islands of Immortals: China-Japan Relations in the Han-Tang Period*. Honolulu: Association for Asian Studies & University of Hawai'i Press.

Wengrow, D. (2011). 'Archival' and 'sacrificial' economies in Bronze Age Eurasia: an interactionist approach to the hoarding of metals. In T. C. Wilkinson, S. Sherratt & J. Bennet, eds., *Interweaving Worlds: Systemic Interactions in Eurasia, 7th to the 1st Millennia BC*. Oxford: Oxbow, pp. 135–44.

Westerdahl, C. (2015). Sails and the cognitive roles of Viking age ships. In J. H. Barrett & S. J. Gibbon, eds., *Maritime Societies of the Viking and Medieval World*. Leeds: Maney, pp. 14–24.

White, J. A., Burgess, G. H., Nakatsukasa, M., Hudson, M. J., Pouncett, J., Kusaka, S., Yoneda, M., Yamada, Y. & Schulting, R. J. (2021). 3000-year-old shark attack victim from Tsukumo shell-mound, Okayama, Japan. *Journal of Archaeological Science: Reports*, 38, 103065.

White, J. C., & Hamilton, E. (2009). The transmission of early Bronze Age technology to Thailand: new perspectives. *Journal of World Prehistory*, 22, 357–97.

Wilkin, S. Miller, A. V., Taylor, W. T. T. et al. (2020). Dairy pastoralism sustained eastern Eurasian steppe populations for 5000 years. *Nature Ecology & Evolution*, 4, 346–55.

Woo, J.-P. (2018). Interactions between Paekche and Wa in the third to sixth centuries AD based on patterns of trade and exchange. In M. E. Byington, K. Sasaki & M. T. Bale, eds., *Early Korea–Japan Interactions*. Cambridge, MA: Korea Institute, Harvard University, pp. 183–230.

Wright, D. C. (2005). Nomadic power, sedentary security, and the crossbow. *Acta Orientalia Academiae Scientiarum Hungaricae*, 58, 15–31.

Yanagita, Y. (2020). Wakoku ni okeru hōkei itaishisuzuri to togiishi no shutsu-gen nendai to seisaku gijutsu [The date of appearance and fabrication technology of rectangular flat inkstones in the country of Wa]. *Makimukugaku Kenkyū*, 8, 1–65.

Yasuda, Y. (2008). Climate change and the origin and development of rice cultivation in the Yangtze river basin, China. *Ambio*, 37 (Special Report 14), 502–6.

Yasuda, Y. (2013). Epilogue: the decline of civilization. In Y. Yasuda, ed., *Water Civilization: From Yangtze to Khmer Civilizations*. New York: Springer, pp. 459–64.

Yates, R. D. S. (1999). Early China. In K. Raaflaub and N. Rosenstein, eds., *War and Society in the Ancient and Medieval Worlds: Asia, the Mediterranean, Europe and Mesoamerica*. Cambridge, MA: Center for Hellenic Studies, Harvard University, pp. 7–45.

Young, J. (1958). *The Location of Yamatai: A Case Study in Japanese Historiography, 720–1945*. Baltimore, MD: The Johns Hopkins University Press.

Yu, H., Spyrou, M. A., Karapetian, M., et al. (2020). Paleolithic to Bronze Age Siberians reveal connections with first Americans and across Eurasia. *Cell*, 181(6), 1232–45.

Yü, Y.-S. (1967). *Trade and Expansion in Han China*. Berkeley: University of California Press.

Yuan, J., & Flad, R. (2005). New zooarchaeological evidence for changes in Shang dynasty animal sacrifice. *Journal of Anthropological Archaeology*, 24, 252–70.

Zancan, C. (2013). Decorated Tombs in Southwest Japan: Behind the Identity and the Socio-political Developments of the Late Kofun Society in Kyushu. MA thesis, Faculty of Archaeology, University of Leiden.

Zhang, C., & Hung, H.-C. (2010). The emergence of agriculture in southern China. *Antiquity*, 84, 11–25.

Zvelebil, M. (1995). Indo-European origins and the agricultural transition in Europe. *Journal of European Archaeology*, 3(1), 33–71.

Acknowledgements

I thank Rowan Flad and Erica Brindley for inviting me to write this Element. As well as the series editors, two anonymous reviewers provided detailed and much-appreciated comments on the text. I also thank Peter Bellwood, John Breen, Seiji Kobayashi and Takeo Kusumi for replying to questions about aspects of the manuscript and Junzō Uchiyama for preparing many of the illustrations.

Over the years, many teachers, friends, students and colleagues – some sadly no longer with us – have contributed in various ways to the ideas developed here. I would especially like to thank Yoshihiko Amino, Bruce Batten, Ilona Bausch, Andrej Bekeš, Izumi Braddick, Miha Budja, Walter Edwards, Garrett Fagan, Linda Fibiger, Ben Fitzhugh, Dorian Fuller, Simon Kaner, Takamune Kawashima, J. Edward Kidder, Toshihiko Kikuchi, Kristian Kristiansen, Takehiko Matsugi, Naoko Matsumoto, Kōji Mizoguchi, Tessa Morris-Suzuki, Masaaki Okita, Seiji Nakayama, Igor de Rachewiltz, Rick Schulting, Takurō Segawa, Mathew Spriggs, Hiroto Takamiya and Alyssa White. In Jena, I am grateful to my colleagues at the Max Planck Institute for the Science of Human History, in particular to Martine Robbeets and Nicole Boivin for providing such a welcoming work environment. Last but not least, I thank Danièle for her critical Renaissance eye and support.

The research leading to these results has received funding from the European Research Council (ERC) under the European Union's Horizon 2020 research and innovation programme (grant agreement No. 646612).

I dedicate this Element to my teachers who gave me a Eurasian perspective: K. N. Chaudhuri, Gina Barnes and Peter Bellwood.

Cambridge Elements ☰

Elements in Ancient East Asia

Erica Fox Brindley

Pennsylvania State University

Erica Fox Brindley is Professor and Head in the Department of Asian Studies at Pennsylvania State University. She is the author of three books, co-editor of several volumes, and the recipient of the ACLS Ryskamp Fellowship and Humboldt Fellowship. Her research focuses on the history of the self, knowledge, music, and identity in ancient China, as well as on the history of the Yue/Viet cultures from southern China and Vietnam.

Rowan Kimon Flad

Harvard University

Rowan Kimon Flad is the John E. Hudson Professor of Archaeology in the Department of Anthropology at Harvard University. He has authored two books and over 50 articles, edited several volumes, and served as editor of *Asian Perspectives*. His archaeological research focuses on economic and ritual activity, interregional interaction, and technological and environmental change, in the late Neolithic and early Bronze Ages of the Sichuan Basin and the Upper Yellow River valley regions of China.

About the Series

Elements in Ancient East Asia contains multi-disciplinary contributions focusing on the history and culture of East Asia in ancient times. Its framework extends beyond anachronistic, nation-based conceptions of the past, following instead the contours of Asian sub-regions and their interconnections with each other. Within the series there are five thematic groups: 'Sources', which includes excavated texts and other new sources of data; 'Environments', exploring interaction zones of ancient East Asia and long-distance connections; 'Institutions', including the state and its military; 'People', including family, gender, class, and the individual and 'Ideas', concerning religion and philosophy, as well as the arts and sciences. The series presents the latest findings and strikingly new perspectives on the ancient world in East Asia.

Cambridge Elements ≡

Elements in Ancient East Asia

Elements in the Series

Violence and the Rise of Centralized States in East Asia
Mark Edward Lewis

Bronze Age Maritime and Warrior Dynamics in Island East Asia
Mark Hudson

A full series listing is available at: www.cambridge.org/ECTP

Printed in the United States
by Baker & Taylor Publisher Services